Praise for Positive Community:
Columns from the Peterborough Examiner 2015-2018

Rosemary's ability to illuminate the issues we are concerned about is a phenomenon we can all be proud of, not just here in Peterborough, but everywhere in our country. She edifies as she incites us to work for justice, work for a better world, and remember that action, on all fronts, is necessary. Joe Webster, Curriculum Chair, English, St. Peter Catholic Secondary School

I read Rosemary Ganley's columns with delight. In a world where I feel bombarded by news that is fearful and horrifying, hers is a voice that articulates kindness, firmness, intelligence and compassion. She finds all of them active and alive in my own city, and in the farflung places of her travels. So, instead of a sleepwalk into despair, these essays challenge the reader, often with humour, to open the inner eye. Margaret Slavin, Quaker Meeting of Peterborough

Rosemary Ganley's articles are gems for Peterborough and for social justice. Her gifts in uncovering issues, bringing life to them through personal stories, and leading people to action creates inspiration for her readers. We thank Rosemary for sharing these articles in this lasting collection. Casey Ready, PhD, Author, "Shelter in a Storm: Revitalizing Feminism in Neoliberal Ontario" and Executive Director, Community Counselling & Resource Centre

Rosemary Ganley takes the pulse of a community, writes of movements that further growth and transformation, and brings to our attention caring people, people of compassion and service to the marginalized. Her articles challenge us to see more clearly and act more selflessly in a great community. We are all richer as we read her column every week. Fr Leo Coughlin, Priest-Counsellor, Peterborough

Rosemary is an inspiration to all of us. A Peterborough icon, she speaks the truth, even if the content is unsettling. She is a role model for women of all ages, and we are proud to claim Rosemary as one of our 'women of influence.' Anne Morawetz, Co-Director, Camp Ponacka, Peterborough

Rosemary Ganley shines a penetrating but always loving light on what gives a community heart. Her writing is lively, her thinking critical and her point of view fearless. Cheryl Lyon, Transition Town Peterborough

June 13/18

& all started
& think with
you us!

Rosemary

Positive Community

Columns from the Peterborough Examiner 2015-2018

ROSEMARY GANLEY

YELLOW DRAGONFLY PRESS

Peterborough, Ontario, Canada

Positive Community:
Columns from the Peterborough Examiner 2015-2018
Copyright ©2018 Rosemary Ganley

Published by *Yellow Dragonfly Press*
www.yellowdragonflypress.ca

Photo Credits ~
Front Cover - Rosemary Ganley at Harper Park 2017 © Robert Hood
Page 13 - Rosemary Ganley © Jessica Melnick for the Red Pashmina Campaign
Back Cover - Trillium near Trent University, 2007 © Robert Hood

Editorial & Book Design ~ Pegi Eyers, Stone Circle Press **www.stonecirclepress.com**

Disclaimer: Any errors and shortcomings in this discourse are my own.
Some columns may not have complete attribution, for which I apologize.

Library and Archives Canada Cataloguing in Publication

Ganley, Rosemary
Positive Community: Columns from the Peterborough Examiner 2015-2018
ISBN-13: 978-1986995443
ISBN-10: 1986995445

Maryam Monsef, Rosemary Ganley
and Carolyn Bennett

Rosemary Ganley at work

Contents

Columns 2015

Columns 2016

Columns 2017

Columns 2018

Foreword

When Rosemary Ganley approached me to discuss writing a regular column for *The Examiner's* opinion page, my response was something like, "Why didn't I think of this before?"

Rosemary and I had known each other for a few years through the paper's coverage of, and her involvement in, various causes, events and community issues. The organization she co-founded, Jamaican Self-Help, had a high profile. She ran for city council. She turned up everywhere and occasionally wrote a series of columns for us during her fascinating global travels.

Her timing was perfect. We were in the midst of change here in the newsroom, with new writers, new reporters and new guy (me) at the helm. Some of our established columnists had moved on, and I was looking to switch things up a bit.

The majority of our national columnists were, at the time, chosen by Sun Media, our owner back then, and they tended to have a certain slant. I was in the process of recruiting a few new people when Rosemary popped in one day and made her pitch.

It made perfect sense. No general theme, no single focus, no agenda - just a regular column on life in Rosemary Ganley's world. Her topics have ranged from abortion and the Catholic church to women's issues and the modern polarization in politics – along with clever, often funny musings on travel, weather and quilting, and profiles of fascinating people.

The columns vary in topic and tone, but they consistently reflect the reasons why people love Rosemary Ganley - her sense of social justice, her firm understanding of what's right and what's wrong, her deep-rooted compassion for all people (even those who don't share her views) and her wish to see Peterborough (and Ontario, and Canada) become even better.

Kennedy Gordon
Managing Editor
The Peterborough Examiner

Introduction

This is a collection of over 100 newspaper columns I have written from 2015-2018, which were published in *The Peterborough Examiner*. They reflect my thinking and also have shaped it, as I got to know my city even more deeply and tried to tell its unique stories.

Having a voice gives meaning to one's life.

It all began I think, in 1994, when I was teaching high school English classes at St. Peter's Secondary School in Peterborough. A cheeky young lad said to me with a smile, "Mrs Ganley, you are always giving us writing assignments. They give us grief! Do you yourself do some too?"

That's a good question for a teacher of writing, who has the "power" to require others to do the work of thinking and writing and correcting and submitting for judgment. Even though we teachers encouraged young writers, and posted and printed good student work, there was an unequal dynamic at work, which he had pointed to.

Then at a post-grad course for teachers, I heard a professor urge us to do the same: write, submit to publications and learn from the results.

I had written sporadically in the years previously, in my own high school paper and in teachers college: some short fiction and even a bit of poetry. But more, I was drawn to opinion piece as an active observer of my community and of the wider society.

I had been raised in a family of "small-p" political participants, living in a small Northern town, but also considering myself involved in bigger questions. Family discussions were lively: my father subscribed in the fifties to Hansard, the daily record of the House of Commons. It came every week in the mail, a newsprint copy. And he read it, actually following what MPs said!

As a result, I absorbed the confidence to watch, judge and then express myself about issues. I was aware Canada existed in a larger world. I longed to see some of that world. I read a lot. We had no internet, no social media, even no TV, but there was the reassurance of the solid thump of a newspaper landing daily on the front steps.

Thus the natural destination for my 650-word pieces was the local newspaper, that time-honoured instrument of community-building and news reporting and critical opinion.

So it continues, *The Examiner* producing hard copies daily and getting millions of hits on its website every month, having survived the closure of many similar-sized newspapers.

Thank you to editor Kennedy Gordon for his quiet encouragement and for writing the forward to this book. I think sometimes he hears in me the voice of his mother!

Thank you to collaborator Pegi Eyers, herself a writer of note, for her editing, artwork, coaching and layout work.

Thank you to the people of my city who have shared their work, their passions and their commitments. I hope you enjoy all the good that is around us.

Rosemary Ganley
May 1, 2018
Peterborough, Ontario

The Columns

SPARK Brightens up Peterborough
April 9, 2015

Me, I have never been able to take a decent photo. I know that 30 trillion pictures are taken every year, now that digital technology makes it so easy. I even saw on TV a woman who admits she's got a little addiction: she has 30,000 pictures saved on her computer.

But as I go, I scribble and make notes, and some talented creative person, such as a Clifford Skarsted, takes the shots. Still, though I can't photograph myself, I know the power of a photo to alter minds, move hearts, and drive action.

For example, in 1973, war photographer Nick Ut was in Vietnam. He captured a searing shot of a ten-year-old Vietnamese girl named Kim Phuc, running, desperate and naked from her village, her back aflame with napalm. That photo, flashed around the world, has been credited with bringing the Vietnam war to an end. I also know the work of Annie Leibowitz, who has taken riveting pictures of women who have had mastectomies, and found glory in the human body. Who can forget Chris Hadfield's pictures of our vulnerable, beautiful blue planet?

With genuine appreciation then, I see the work of SPARK, a community-based Peterborough photo festival, just in its third year. It is really quite astonishing. The brainchild of photo lovers Micky Renders, Bill Lockington and Rob Boudreau, SPARK took flight just a year and a half after the first meeting of these three.

15

Attracting over fifty photographers, amateur and professional, with a curated and judged competition for some, and a children's workshop program, SPARK lasts all of April. Every exhibition is free to the public. Each photographer goes about finding a location to show his or her work. Local businesses are happy to oblige. They clear wall space. They paint. They plan opening receptions. The SPARK organizers print up a glossy catalogue and brochures, showing where all these photos will be shown. Salute to volunteer Alan Brunger, a Trent geographer who did up the map, which will get me places.

I happen to know that Jamaican Self-Help participates. Its colourful Caribbean scenes, all taken by Peterborough volunteers in Jamaica, are hanging in Naked Chocolate, its neighbour on Hunter Street, a business run by Warren Eley and Angela Roest.

Venues for showing photos include Chasing the Cheese, Frame it for You, the YMCA, the Canadian Canoe Museum, Dreams of Beans, Elements Restaurant and the Tourism Visitor Centre. Let's not forget the Bridgenorth Public Library and the Airport Terminal.

In a wildly original endeavor, SPARK will open the month on April 1 with an exhibition of seventy of the photos of writer Lucy Maud Montgomery at the Old YMCA. Montgomery, famous author of *Anne of Green Gables*, moved to Ontario from PEI and followed her passion for photography. She bought a small camera with her first teaching paycheque in 1880. The pictures have been loaned by the University of Guelph. We can see them starting April 1.

SPARK is another unique Peterborough success story: a very small budget, raised by donations, registration fees, corporate sponsors, and advertisers in the catalogue. It has attracted attention from all across Ontario.

Community-building is its lasting effect, as artists meet business people, and all of us relish their work.

16

Not long ago, I was at a photo gathering of Peterborough bike enthusiasts......the cyclers who love the outdoors and save the planet at the same time. I imagine these photographers are imbued with the same passion for beauty, conservation and meditation.

They are the leaders of the change in consciousness we need today.

Homestead Theatre Flourishes
July 23, 2015

For most of the civic groups I know, those who seek to engage the public or raise money for good causes, turn-out is always the crucial and worrying factor. All those bake sales, annual general meetings, rallies and marches, church services, service club efforts and cultural endeavours: the question is always: how many will come?

We fret about our message getting out to the public, about the competing lure of computers and televisions, about the fatigue and the cost factors.

So we look with awe and admiration at a small local theatre project on Tara Road in Ennismore, called Ennismore Homestead Theatre. It scarcely publicizes, has no advertising budget, sells no tickets online, and yet has long lineups on the summer morning when its seats go on sale. Limited, now, to six per person.

What it has in abundance is talent, creativity, a strong sense of identity, knowledge of its audience, musicianship and a rollicking sense of fun. It also has a barn-full of good local actors who make their living elsewhere than professional theatre, but will give some summer time to rehearsals and performances for the good of the community. Think Jane Werger, former drama teacher at St Peter's, Jerry Allen, award-winning Ontario director, Kevin O'Neill, teacher and droll comic performer, and gifted amateurs such as Marian Stewart, Newfoundland-born exemplar of Newfie accents for whole casts.

Homestead Theatre has two powerful factors working in its favour: the immense energy and talent of playwright-founder Paul Crough, whose day job is in the drama department of St Peter's Secondary School, and the loyalty of his audience, who have been vastly moved and entertained for the past five years. His colleague and former teacher Jane Werger, who acts this summer in *More Than a Memory*, has directed three of Paul's plays at Homestead.

Crough sings, composes, researches and writes scripts and scores, directs and acts and produces. Perhaps most importantly, he has talked his sister and brother-in-law in Ennismore, Kendra and Todd Willis, into giving over their family barn for performances every summer. All in the family. I remember Paul as a high school student leader. I remember his going off to sing with *Up With People* in the nineties. UWP continues to be a global education and goodwill organization headquartered in Denver, whose casts of musical young people travel to communities on several continents over a semester, to live with a local family, entertain and do volunteer work. I remember Paul's memorable turn in the recent production in Peterborough of *Les Miserables*.

His plays explore various themes and settings. This theatre is local but universal too: about memory, loss, regret, resilience, laughter and love.

If what Canadians most need is a sense of place to combat modern rootlessness, look no further than regional story-telling. Years ago, Northrop Frye, the great New Brunswick scholar, said to Margaret Laurence, we must write out of our own place.

The 2015 offering, opening July 22 and running for 17 performances is *More Than a Memory*. The first five years were devoted to comedies. This year, says Crough, the play has a darker hue, set in Donegal at the end of the First World War.

When it closes, he will be busy writing again. He collaborates for the music over the internet with other musicians, mostly from the Maritimes.

What is interesting, is that the more we Canadians are subjected to full-blown shows meant to dazzle, the more we crave homey, accessible and intimate plays with feeling. That niche Homestead fills admirably.

And by the way, Homestead Theatre is non-profit. Now there's a pioneering notion.

Dismantle Democracy and Disdain the People
August 20, 2015

My July column about Homestead Theatre in Ennismore was a "feel-good" one. That's what one experiences, on emerging from the barn on Tara Road after a laugh-filled evening of local theatre.

This month I am dark, after reading a report on Canada today compiled by a respected, five-year-old group of smart Canadians called "Voices-Voix." Among them are Alex Neve, the admired head of Amnesty International, Oxfam's Robert Fox, lawyer Mary Eberts from the 1982 Charter of Rights project, and Joanna Kerr of Greenpeace.

These are conscientious, knowledgeable and caring people, not suspects. They have no vested interests. My bias has always been that people at the grassroots are most to be trusted when we try to analyze what is happening to us. No spin-doctors here. No media, no political parties, no institutions.

Canada, where art thou?

Is our educated population asleep, willfully blind or lulled by perks and handouts? Are we dazzled by our country's "reputation," that we are better than most of the world's 200 countries? What then, about the accumulating evidence that this "city on the hill" is sliding rapidly downhill? As a democracy, that is. Outsiders are noticing. "What is happening to Canada?" young Canadian travelers are being asked this summer.

Voices-Voix has researched and written a 65-page report entitled *Dismantling Democracy*. I was shocked when I read it. Carefully, even dispassionately, the paper reviews what the past 10 years have brought us. It is not pretty.

In this long and often crazy election season, perhaps we should all take a careful look. The cover illustration of DD is a picture of our 1982 Charter of Rights, the one hanging in every school. It is eviscerated by scissors.

You bet that we have economic worries to attend to. My young relatives can't get jobs at their skill level either. But ignoring the fact that our capacity to participate in decisions in our society is shrinking, and that we are threatened with punishment for our sometimes contrary views, is truly frightening.

David-Letterman-style then, here are ten charges which Voices-Voix makes, backed up by facts and examples (more next month: it's a long list):

Number 10 Public servants, or "watchdogs" silenced, fired or smeared in public for criticizing official policy. Never mind that that is their job. Think Linda Keen, Canadian Nuclear Safety Commission; Marty Cheliak, Canadian Firearms Program (long gun registry); Deana Allen, Canadian Wheat Board; Paul Kennedy and Marc Mayrand, Elections Canada; Richard Colvin, diplomat; Kevin Page, budget officer; Pat Stogran, veterans advocate. And plenty more.

Number 9 Hostility to science that is at odds with government policy. The ordering of government scientists not to talk to media. Holy moly, that is an attack on free-flowing knowledge, in my book. Information I might like to consider. Data that might wisely guide decisions: about the environment, about medicines, about trends in our population.

Number 8 The permanent attitude that critics are enemies. So strangle their independence by oppressive audits, then demonize and exclude them from national dialogue.

In the case of the highly suspicious Bill C51, which greatly increases surveillance of us, don't even let the Canadian Bar Association itself come before a committee. Be at war with citizens everywhere, all the time. Cut the CBC, which strives mightily to carry out its mandate to inform, to strengthen our national consciousness, to be independent and therefore critical. Marginalize individuals who advocate for environmental action or scientific transparency.

Number 7 Eliminate the Canadian International Development Agency and reduce international development to its lowest levels since is beginning: (2.3% of GDP), and then fold it into trade. Mining companies are fit to do human development in poor countries? Puh-lease.

Tie foreign aid programs tightly to far-right ideology, such as the Maternal and Child Health package excluding reproductive health services.

Number 6 Ram through scores of disparate pieces of legislation in "Omnibus Bills." In 2010, it was 880 pages long. Prevent opposition examination of them.

Number 5 Devalue Indigenous voices; refuse inquiry into the complex national problem of violence towards Indigenous women.

A dreary list for sure, but one we absolutely must examine in the next seven weeks. More on the top ten next month.

Tilting Towards a Meaner Canada
September 17, 2015

Are you still with me, readers? My usual goal, as a friendly columnist, is to cheer and entertain you. After all, Peterborough brims with good-news stories. But this election season, only once every four years, it seems important to comment on the *Dismantling Democracy* report from a coalition of concerned Canadians called "Voices-Voix."

It lists major offenses against democracy which have been committed in Canada in the last ten years.

It's not even about policy, it's about process: the diminishing avenues for us to participate, and if we do criticize, to get ready for a hit. Not the historic Canadian way. Sixty-five percent of us are perceiving the direction and are uneasy. Did you see the Toronto artist and writer team who recently created a cotton bag emblazoned "My Prime Minister Embarrasses Me" in French and English? Sold out in a day.

David Letterman-style, the dismal list might run:

Number 4 Practice contempt for Parliament by proroguing or cancelling it four times since 2006. The first was to prevent a non-confidence vote from taking place; the second to prevent the House receiving a report on abuse of Afghan prisoners by the Canadian military; the third to prevent a report on misuse of public money by senators. We in Peterborough have suffered through almost a year of no representation at all in Ottawa. A neighbouring politician with a thin understanding of representative democracy, said, "What's wrong? You can still get passports."

Number 3 Work from the premise that there is no such thing as society, just individuals striving to make their own way. That's a discredited Margaret Thatcher notion. And it flies in the face of our communitarian spirit. But if you hold it, of what use then is the long-form census to tell us about ourselves as a group?

22

Number 2 Use a national tragedy to justify ramping up surveillance (Bill C51) and curtail civil liberties without adequate oversight of the agencies who will collect data and watch us. The United Nations itself is concerned about C 51 and our liberties. Pulitzer prize- winning author Chris Hedges, a respected American journalist, says shocked, "We have nothing like it even in the States."

Number 1 For you to name.

May I add a few Ganley "Bonus Offences?"

Ghastly, self-serving appointments.

Recently the appointment of Steven Kelly, who is a Kinder Morgan oil executive, to the very panel which regulates the oil industry, the National Energy Board. Then, the appointment of Russell Brown of Alberta to the Supreme Court. Mr. Brown, as a sitting justice, kept a public blog, in which he slagged Justin Trudeau and even Chief Justice Beverly McLachlin. A judge. A public blog.

These appointments take place with no review, no vetting. You wonder why these men aren't embarrassed by their conflict of interest so blatant.

Never mind the Senate appointments: Brazeau, Duffy and Wallin, or the naming of the unqualified Marc Nadon to the Supreme Court. Never mind the reduction of funds to the National Library, or to the office which responds to Freedom of Information requests. Look at the Board of the CBC, nine members, not one broadcaster and not one educator. Is this our general dumbing-down?

Voices-Voix goes further and connects the dots: it sees creeping authoritarianism, as we slumber on.

In the most terrifying comment, the report quotes University of Ottawa professor of constitutional law, Dr Errol Mendes saying of these interferences with democratic institutions, oversight agencies and the public service:

"This abuse of executive power is tilting towards totalitarian government, and away from the foundations of democracy and the rule of law, on which his country was founded."

This is the dreaded "T" word. Such a tilt we must recognize and stop.

Pope Has a Blind Spot When it Comes to Women October 15, 2015

I'm frequently drawn to ponder the Pope question.

Not from the point of view of the pious, even of the believer, but from the point of view of global politics, politics being all about power. And influence.

Recently I was in Philadelphia, the city of "brotherly love." That's where the first U.S. Constitution was composed, debated and adopted in 1776. It has some sacred sites for Americans: Independence Hall and the Liberty Bell, and the home of Betsy Ross, the seamstress who made the first Stars and Stripes.

Philly was agog about the coming papal visit (Sept 25-27). Flags and photos and souvenirs everywhere. Huge banners on lampposts with some of his sayings: "We are all called to have the courage to be happy."

In most shops, papal merchandise elbowed out that of the baseball Phillies. Adoring crowds and fawning TV anchors and insider commentators. Not a word of analysis or criticism.

I went to the historic McGillin's Pub, founded in 1860. In addition to NFL games roaring out from six walls, there was a life-sized cardboard cutout of Pope Francis, with which everyone was posing. Me too.

But at a nearby hotel, 500 feminist Catholic women from all over the world met for three days to prepare a critique of Pope Francis' positions on women and on sexual matters. At my table were women from Sri Lanka, Mexico and New Zealand. I called a "Canadian Caucus," and 22 women came: from Ottawa, Kingston, Guelph, Brockville, Regina, Sudbury. Some spouses too.

The women's gathering recognized that Pope Francis is a fine man, generous and humble, and has issued radically wonderful statements on the environment and on rapacious capitalism. My "green" friends have been saying to me: "Can't you just write an unqualified rave about his letter on climate?"

No, I simply can't.

Because what many of us see is a serious, confused, blind spot regarding women. Some shrink in horror at things the Pope has said: that women are the "strawberries on the cake," that women are complementary to men but different in essence, and that the issue of the ordination of women to priesthood is a "closed door."

He just doesn't seem able to recognize the full humanity of women or to connect the issues: poverty around the world is endured mostly by women and children, control of fertility is crucial to the struggle to rise, to say nothing of managing overpopulation, and that church misogyny can be related to violence against women.

Second-class status for women imposed by a global power like the Roman Catholic Church coupled with 19th century sexual doctrines, makes a toxic potion that is exploited by chauvinists in all countries. It becomes an excuse and a justification for their own policies of discrimination.

In Philadelphia, the Pope condemned contraception, abortion, in-vitro fertilization and same-sex marriage as "sins, tragedies and threats to the faith." This is all damage done to the common good. How much more powerful would Francis' calls for equality and justice be, if the church itself were a true reflection of justice and equality?

For Catholic feminists, it is a long, hard struggle. In 1979, Sr. Theresa Kane stood to chastise Pope John Paul II on this very matter. He sat stone-faced. Now fully 36 years later, Theresa Kane, frail and feisty, read her statement for Pope Francis. She called the treatment of women a scandal to church and world.

Can this leader listen and learn and lead? That is the question now.

Stop the press: Women are hailing a speech in Rome Oct 6 by Archbishop Paul-Andre Durocher of Gatineau, PQ, calling for women to be ordained deacons.

Progress, glacial, but progress.

The Crushing of Jamaican Self-Help
November 16, 2015

This column is full of sadness and anger. Maybe you should skip to the sports pages (Raptors?).

On October 10, the occasion of its 35th anniversary in Peterborough and in Jamaica, the international development organization founded here 35 years ago, Jamaican Self-Help, announced its forced closure as of June, 2016. Its office on Hunter Street will close at end of January.

"This is terrible news, terrible," said Professor Haroon Akram-Lodhi of Trent International Development Studies.

Forced because of a funding shortfall brought about by a regressive federal policy begun in 2012, without consultation with Canadians, to decrease our aid budget to a parsimonious 0.2% of gross domestic product (Britain's is 0.7%), and to get rid of CIDA and to defund small community organizations, in favour of putting human development in the hands of mining companies overseas.

Full disclosure here: I have been involved with JSH since its beginning.

Canada has become one of the world's worst-performing aid donors. You can imagine the feelings of betrayal of the once-thriving network of Canadian agencies, at one time about 700 in number. They have been small, real, honest and effective. Just as important has been the engagement in their work taken up by thousands of Canadians of all walks of life. They have organized, fundraised, donated, spoken out, and educated their fellow citizens.

At JSH, for example, there have been 1000 volunteers, almost all youth, to have had a service experience in Jamaica, which has shaped their views, their commitments and their values.

Cutting support from the smaller NGOs to 100 of the larger ones, has become a betrayal of Canadians interested in working for world peace and prosperity. It denies the data that effectiveness lies in long-term aid. It enrages all those involved in the work by offering a specious rationale: Canada should benefit economically from all arrangements.

Canada has gone back on its 2009 pledge to put poverty reduction at the forefront of all assistance. We began to pick middle-income countries, such as Peru and Colombia, where our extraction companies are at work.

The umbrella organization, the Canadian Council for International Co-operation, which linked up small NGOs, encouraged them to sign a Code of Ethics and gave them "best practice" education, was cut savagely. The government, so ideologically driven, didn't like criticism from any civil society group. And the Minister, Julian Fantino wasn't equipped to grasp the issues or defend the NGOs.

27

Glowing evaluations of JSH, dating back to its first matching support year, 1983, (that's 29 years of funding), counted for nothing. At $200,000 a year, this match was small but crucial to JSH.

JSH has striven for two years to make up the shortfall. Letting down the partners in Kingston, Jamaica was the first sorrow. Suzanne Smith, manager of St Margaret's Human Resource Centre in inner-city Kingston who was in Peterborough for the anniversary, found it in herself to comfort JSH'ers. "Don't fret," she said, "you have helped us so much." JSH supported woodworking training there, as young men rebuilt their lives, got skills and eshewed crime and drugs.

The JSH timeline goes like this:

1976-87: a few Peterborough volunteers bring the "singing priest", Fr Richard Ho Lung and his group for delightful, sold-out concerts, and his talks about the poverty in their country. Many Peterburians respond.

1980: Jamaican Self Help is incorporated. $25,000 is raised the first year for inner-city women's housing. JSH learns early to listen, really listen, to its partners in the ghettos. One early request is for help building a wall around a poor and violent one-block, community. A wall? Yes, the answer comes, to keep the pigs out who are giving the children diseases, and to keep out the gunmen who run through the block, guns blazing, the police in hot pursuit. JSH gets it.

1984: Awareness trips for youth begin. In the ensuing years young people serve as tutors in literacy programs at schools and orphanages, and on farms.

1983: CIDA approves the grassroots work and begins to match the funds which JSH raises, 1 to 1. Annual budgets rise to $450,000. A small and talented staff work for frugal wages. Peterborough becomes more progressive, more global and inclusive, and less racist.

For the government of Stephen Harper, this doesn't seem to have been enough. And thus, our community has been greatly diminished and our partners further impoverished.

A Definition of "Edifying"
November 15, 2015

What I saw at the Peterborough New Canadians Centre this week gave new meaning to the word "edifying."

My dictionary, (the Canadian Oxford), says this word means "what improves one morally or intellectually," as in "good."

I came away edified, meditating on the goodness of my neighbours here, "neighbours" in the wide sense.

At the corner of Aylmer and Romaine Streets, above St James United Church, the New Canadians Centre, first started by volunteers in 1979, now ably led by Hajni Hos and featuring 10 multicultural staff members, has welcomed and settled hundreds of immigrants to Peterborough over the years.

But now it is charged with a huge new responsibility, helping prepare the 30 or more local groups who have formed in the past few weeks, some arising just out of neighbourhood friendships, all driven by human solidarity with the suffering of others. People talked together and started the ambitious process of becoming a private sponsor for a refugee family from Syria.

NCC's Tamara Hogerdyk and Michael Vanderherberg prepared a detailed and helpful list of considerations that sponsors need to be thinking and deciding about. It is quite exhaustive. The groups, as small as two persons and as large as 30, must raise between $25,000 and $40,000 depending on the size of "their" family. They are committed to caring for the family for a year or until employment is found. They need to face such thorny issues as who controls the budget for the family, how can temporary housing be arranged so that the family has some autonomy in choosing their home, arranging OHIP cards, registering children in school, arranging phone and internet and language training, finding an interpreter, teaching familiarity with mail, snow shoveling and garbage. And so on.

The two-hour session, peppered by questions, was honest, realistic and laced with examples. Just to mention some of the groups who have felt the urge to come forward, form a committee and plan shelter for a few of the thousands of distraught refugees we have been seeing on our TV screens are these: The Avenues, the Harvey-London-Waterford group, Safe Haven, Hope for Homes, Sacred Heart Church, the Abraham Festival, the Parkhill Road Mosque, Casa Maria, Trent Hills, the Unitarian Fellowship, the United Church of Bobcaygeon, Salaam Peterborough, the Parry Sound Group, and the Brighton Group.

Joe McGuire of Downeyville, a long-time peace and justice activist, amused the crowd as he described standing up at his church, St Luke's, and saying bluntly, "We aren't going to do bake sales for $27,000. There are 170 members in this parish. I need each of you to give me a cheque for $100!"

The amazing thing is that it all came in. Joe thinks small communities are very effective at such charity when they put their minds to it. The Peterborough mosque will welcome people who want to know more about Islam.

The groups receive a profile of their family in advance. There were gasps of pleasure when one group said, "Our family speaks some English!" Another brave group said, "We have a single mother and six kids."

What these committees will need to endure now in the face of the outrages in Paris, will be increased opposition to sponsorship. Links will be made between the suffering of Paris and the refugee crisis. One hopes that the voices being heard against our national effort to give succor to people, people who have been carefully vetted and living in camps in Lebanon and Jordan for a long time, will mute themselves, knowing that the refugees are fleeing the same terror that has assaulted Europe.

In an oblique reference to our recent election, one woman said to me, "It's all right to be nice again. Our natural state."

Hope she is right.

Of Christmas and Causes
December 3, 2015

I am coming to like December better and better these days.

For one, the weather forecasters are calling for a warm winter ahead, with lots of snow, which pleases just about everyone I know, especially the cross-country skiers.

For another, I may have learned at long last to simplify. To reduce anxiety and fatigue. I have 14 close family members, including eight grandchildren under 15 years of age. Mailing a book or small parcel to Edmonton, for example, now costs a whopping $14. That is really out of the question. So, I learn about online shopping and free delivery. About greeting cards with a handy slot for a cheque. And about gift cards for Cineplex and Chapters and even the beer store.

In return, I mention to my busy and generous sons that they can keep an account at Libby's Kitchen or BE Catering here in Peterborough, and have me a casserole delivered. Wonderful for the indifferent cook. I then can make a salad and have people over and present it as my own.

It seems I can avoid the malls pretty well completely. There is so much falsely cheerful music and advertising and excess, just at a time when our mood is understandably often dark. More consuming, every year. Is the joy in all this on a level with the stress? I understand with recognition that it is all motivated by love, one for another. But on a small planet under threat, how much more plastic does one need?

Good grief, Pope Francis himself called today for a greatly reduced Christmas "in a world with so much war."

In trying to change my old excessive December habits, I find I must substitute for shopping some meaningful experiences of peace and joy, in order to stay strong and at times, counter-cultural.

That's where our community offers many actions for justice. Actually, one can begin early, on November 29, with the March for the Climate, starting at Trinity Church at 2 pm.

Worldwide, there will be hundreds of such public gatherings to give some muscle to the upcoming climate talks in Paris. There, December 1-11, heads of state will meet to hammer out, we hope, a really meaningful commitment to lowering carbon emissions. May their work be a tribute to all the innocent lives taken on November 13.

December 6 is the day we remember the Montreal massacre in 1989, in which 14 women were shot. The YWCA, which works day in and day out helping local women fleeing violence, will not have a public gathering this year, but asks people to remember the day by taking part in their "Wrapped in Courage" campaign, by which one visits the Y on Simcoe Street and purchases a purple scarf for $15. I can do that. Dislodging misogyny and male privilege will be a long tough struggle, many more years in the achieving.

On December 10, Amnesty International, on whose national board I sat for two years, holds its public letter-writing session at the Whistle Stop Café on George Street from 4 to 6 pm. The social justice class of Trevor Digby at Holy Cross wrote letters last week. It is heartening to see humble people come in out of the cold, pick up information on a case of human rights abuse somewhere in the world, and sit down to write a letter or a card to the victim or to the authorities holding this person. Maybe do three more, and then slip away. The evidence shows that these letters matter.

And one can have a celebratory dish of poutine!

As the month progresses, there will be in this city and county a multitude of kind acts, community dinners and gift baskets delivered to the needy. A benefit for the Warming Room with local musicians, comes on December 20 at The Venue.

For quiet and inspiration, there is much choral music everywhere. And there are the poems of Mary Oliver.

December is all of this.

Joyeux Noel, Salaam Alaikum, and Happy Hanukkah (December 6-14).

A Swearing-in on Parliament Hill
December 17, 2015

It all began quietly a few years back, when spouse John introduced me to a young Peterborough woman named Maryam. She had an international interest, as we did, and a project to help Afghanistan.

Little did I know. Never in my wildest dreams did I think I would be having such a gala ride in late 2015: euphoric about our country's new direction, able to resist the naysayers, having waited a long, long, time for this fresh wave, and having been given an invitation to attend Maryam's swearing-in as MP for Peterborough.

That meant asking Jenn Harrington, who had been Maryam's scheduler, to take me along, with her two school-age kids to Ottawa. The security there is more noticeable now and there are alternative entrances to the main one and a frisking takes place, but the personnel are affable all the same. They had our names ahead of time.

It is a finely-wrought room, the Railway Committee Room, with its high ceilings and space for perhaps 400 chairs on the second floor of the grand Centre Block building. There were 30 other family and friends. The room features a colourful copy of the famous painting of the Fathers of Confederation meeting in 1867: a gathering of men (size: 365 by 213 cm), that just underscores how far we women have come. We strove to include the painting in the candid photos each of us took with our newly-sworn MP.

Painter Robert Harris did the original picture in 1882. It shows 23 male delegates and a male secretary. Our first Prime Minister, John A Macdonald, is standing. The original was destroyed in a lamented parliamentary fire of February, 1916, when seven people perished. They were mostly women from the public galleries who had stopped at the coat check to claim their belongings. All but our National Library, at the rear of the Centre Block, went up in flames.

The story goes that our alert librarian, when fire alarms sounded, slammed shut the heavy iron doors to the library and saved the collection. The doors are still there. The library has a million books and documents, but it is now also digitized.

All this Canadian history which I present to you, I picked up during the fascinating 40-minute tour of Parliament and the library which Maryam had arranged. I think now that these tours are largely wasted on the 12-year-olds who trip there every spring with their teachers. It is we seniors who lap it up. Patriots and survivors!

Then the swearing-in and the solo pictures, (this is the "selfie" government, remember), with Maryam. That young woman showed again her sensitivity: with me, she whispered, "This is for John." Of course that smeared my makeup.

On the fifth floor of Centre Block is the three-room office of the Minister of Democratic Institutions, where we had a little reception. I have read her mandate letter from the PM, it is quite a load: Senate reform and electoral processes. It demonstrates his belief in her abilities.

In Confederation Hall, decorated for the season with wreaths and a huge tree lit in red, we spotted CBC radio "Metro Morning" host, Matt Galloway, in very casual clothes. His producer Jessica Low was with him. I always honour and notice producers. These are the "idea" people who make it all happen on air.

Matt had just changed from his suit because he had interviewed the Prime Minister, who that very evening, was on his way to meet the Queen. Matt was pleased to meet Maryam's mother, Soraya, and their picture, all smiles, appeared on the *Metro Morning* website next day.

Said "Hi!" to Minister of Trade, Krystia Freeland too, as we wandered, but she didn't know us. She's from Toronto.

Former Liberal candidate Betsy McGregor, who had worked on the campaigns of several winning women, took me in hand to enjoy the sculpture group just to the east of the Parliament Buildings, which features the western women, the "Famous Five" who successfully launched the case for women as persons in 1929. I hope the school kids do see it.

Enroute home, we had car trouble and were helped immediately by two passersby: a paramedic and a mechanic.

That's what I call a complete Canadian day.

The Beautiful New Face of Peterborough in Ottawa
December 24, 2015

Who would'a thunk it?

That good, old, grey, middle-of-the-road, working-class Peterborough, usually known for its sports fans, plentiful beer joints, dull city councils, and worst of all, eight long years of a wholly unsuitable, even criminal, Member of Parliament, should be sending to Ottawa a young woman who first arrived here in 1996 as a refugee from Afghanistan.

A Muslim, a feminist, an arts graduate, the daughter of a widow who has taught Afghani cooking to support herself while raising three daughters. A young woman whose father was killed in the Russian invasion of her country; who came speaking no English, who credits PCVS and the New Canadian Centre and then Trent University with helping and encouraging her as she grew up.

Who discovered leadership in herself and began to live it out, forming a NGO to help women in her native country, "The Red Pashmina" campaign with her friend, Jess Melnik.

35

Who joined the YWCA Board and represented it in New York at the Status of Women conference of the UN. Who possesses a quiet confidence and ran for mayor, almost unseating the incumbent.

Who was then sought by two political parties to become their candidate for the federal election of 2015 and chose the Liberals, to their everlasting good luck.

Maryam Monsef first came to my attention when my spouse, John, about eight years ago, came home and said, "I'd like to learn more about Islam. I'm going to the Eid Dinner at Trent." I was too tired to go. He came home to say, "I met a fantastic young woman selling red scarves, so I bought ten!"

Maryam's energy and intelligence began to show as she learned the issues, encountered the people with great concentration, made use of her ever-present smart phone, showed a knack for remembering names, paid special attention to youth, attracted 250 volunteers from all ages and walks of life, and showed that our rural areas are just as enlightened as the city centre!

She presented policy at 30 All-Candidates meetings, spent the summer bringing in Liberal leaders: Adam Vaughan, Carolyn Bennett, Marc Garneau, Ralph Goodale and John McKay for engrossing and inclusive roundtables on their area of specialization.

When I look at the country I am jubilant. Is it just the people I hang out with, or is this jubilation as widespread as I think? I have three sons in three different provinces. We talk politics all the time. Edmonton Centre elected Randy Boissenault, a Rhodes scholar. For son Jim, Vancouver Island went all orange, his party, except for Elizabeth May. And we all hail her.

Of course in the nitty-gritty of governing, the jubilation will lessen. But the potential is tremendous. We are out from under, in my view, an increasingly frightening government: authoritarian, ideological, divisive and contemptuous, which had been chipping away at democratic structures for some time.

We have ten aboriginal members, a promise to make the Cabinet gender-equal, and a PM who is taking the premiers to a climate change conference in Paris.

One American friend announces she is moving to Canada. Another says "Ah, I now know what 'riding' means. Thank you, Canada."

Mr Trudeau called on "the better angels of our nature," while campaigning. We did. In Peterborough-Kawartha, 75% of us voted, highest in the country. We are projecting another, more impressive, representative face of our area.

In addition to the splendid candidacy of Monsef, I point to two other citizens who helped turn the tide of national unease into action for rejection: Rick Mercer, of CBC TV, who got the youth vote mobilized, and Tony Turner of Ottawa who wrote the song *Harperman*.

We have the talent and the goodwill to be national leaders. Let's get on with it.

This is My Country, Too
January 7, 2016

There are so many Canadians now with recent pasts in another country. Immigrants, new settlers, family reunifications, refugees.

I believe in this phenomenon, the bringing together of people from all over the world, with its profound sharing of cultures, and the heartening discovery, which is ever new, that we humans are basically alike.

For me, there is also a bit of a reversal. I feel deeply a part of another country, Jamaica. Fate or providence gave me a chance starting in 1975, to live there, in the turbulent capital city of Kingston. To make my way, with uncertainty at first and then with a growing confidence, meeting leaders working hard for the vast numbers of the very poor in their country, joining with them and getting Canadian support for their works.

Of course, there are vast differences between my experience going there with a job offer and a vehicle, and that of a refugee arriving here, desperate and dependent. I could leave at any time. The language was familiar. (No problem!) I had a living wage. Even when I hated having it, I benefitted from white privilege as I went about.

The possibility of being bi-cultural was mine too. And the depth of my attachment to this other country came clear last week when I flew back to Kingston for a funeral.

He was a truly remarkable person, a 69-year-old American Roman Catholic priest from the Bronx named Richard Albert, who, when I met him in the eighties, I would have said had no chance of making it there. He had two bulldogs, a big cigar and a loud voice. I was wrong. What he had in addition to these, was a fierce commitment to the beatitudes. And if one wants to do good, one can certainly find opportunities in Kingston, Jamaica.

At his inner city parishes, people lined up, 50 or 80 a day, to seek his help. He founded two huge community centres, and he was enlightened about what they would offer: skills training, literacy remediation, a woman's centre for pregnant and therefore out-of-school teens, a seniors' feeding program, a legal aid clinic, and a committee for free and fair elections.

He related to inner city "dons," those guys who "run t'ings" outside the law, and to the police and to fugitives. He was featured in a CNN documentary made by the estimable reporter Christiane Ammanpour, and at the end, his obituary appeared in the New York Times.

Richard renounced his US citizenship and became a Jamaican. He had a great sense of humour. He said he worked with the poor but dined with the rich. So all came to his funeral: a former Prime Minister, the wife of the Governor General, the American ambassador, the leader of the Opposition. To my bemusement, I was seated just behind these dignitaries as an "international benefactor." JSH folks here in town will be amused.

By dint of his drive and appeal to conscience, he had literally bound up the nation. So the two-and-a-half hour funeral attracted 2000 people, a Seventh Day Adventist preacher, eight eulogies, singing and clapping, and a sermon by the Minister of Education, who is also a Catholic deacon, Ronnie Thwaites. Church and state are well blended in Jamaica.

When I looked around the church, I could see that the class divide had been bridged by Richard Albert's life and death.

As if to underscore the reality of our bi-cultural potential, I met a woman on the plane home to Toronto. She was Jamaican, but had been in Canada in the Northwest Territories as nurse at the Red Cross outpost at Tsiigehtchic for 16 years. Tsiigehtchic, a Gwich'in hamlet of 200 souls at the confluence of the Mackenzie River and the Arctic Red River, is at 66 degrees north latitude, where today it is minus 30 degrees.

We looked at each deeply and in recognition. Her native country had made me feel at home and, I think, mine had done the same for her.

We had a spontaneous hug.

Dangerous Old Ladies
January 14, 2016

Over at Traill College recently, 50 women, young and old, but mostly old, met for a lively two-day conference examining the impact of their activism on Canadian society.

It was called *Aging Activisms*, the brainchild of Professor May Chazan of Gender and Women's studies, and attended by attentive Trent professors from Political Science and from Literature, and other academics from Concordia, Laurier and the U of T, all interested in charting and analyzing the grassroots activism of older women.

Activists know that, by any name (and they actually prefer "engaged citizens"), they are influential in their families and in the public square, but they are happy that scholars now take an interest in documenting this work. The two groups need each other. It may be a particular talent of the female gender that it can be done so co-operatively.

At least half the participants were some of Peterborough's well-known and admired older women. It was a democratic meeting, with use of music, the arts and popular education techniques.

Maybe it can best take place in small cities such as ours, where women know one another, and have organized many public events, protests, singalongs, and bus trips to Toronto and Ottawa for many years. The activists and the academics benefit mutually from the real-life stories of brave and witty women who take political stands on issues and draw attention, sometimes derision, but usually applause from the public.

To recall just a few actions: in 2012 there was a protest of the repression by police at the G20 meeting in Toronto; in 2002 in Ottawa against the Arms Sales Fair; then a walk (and a drive) in 2001 to Ottawa with the World March of Women; and in 2015, the singing of *Harperman* in Confederation Park.

Older women gathered this October in Millennium Park at a vigil remembering aboriginal women. They mourned once again the deaths in Montreal on December 6. On December 10, they acted with Amnesty International on Human Rights Day. They went to the PRIDE parade and the Take Back the Night walk.

They letter-write too, to the press, to the politicians, to the victims. Some even tweet! There was the astonishingly successful *Calendar Girls* calendar of 2004, which raised $200,000 for flood victims in Peterborough. Older women took the bus to Ottawa in late November to attend the rally organized by the environmental NGO "350.org," to show the new Canadian government the urgency of climate change.

On election day, 85 women (and 15 men) were out for Peterborough's 25th Persons Day Breakfast, where Susan Newman, for the 19th year, sang *Bread and Roses*.

What was refreshing at this conference was the conscious use of down-to-earth terms in describing reality. No more silly euphemisms: the group adopted "old," instead of "elderly" or "senior," and "die" instead of "pass."

Humour has been essential in political women's work. The "Raging Grannies" sang about intimate relationships in old age, and about saving Canada from neo-conservatism. A Manitoba performing artist, Dayna McLeod, showed her film work: honest and a bit raunchy.

There were members of the Older Women's Network, For Our Grandchildren, the Africa-focused Grandmothers Advocacy Network, and Jamaican Self-Help. There was a strong presence of Native women, earth-centered and grounding. Jean Koning, age 93, spoke of her long commitment to solidarity with First Peoples.

Older women have a sense of a personal ending coming, and an urgency to work towards a better future. In a word, they yearn. Long dismissed and patronized in a culture which has lionized youth, old women, smart, seasoned and courageous, come out of a turbulent past but are undaunted by the obstacles ahead.

They like 81-year-old Gloria Steinem's remark: "People ask me when I am going to pass the torch. I am going to keep my torch, thank you very much, but I will be glad to help others light theirs. Because the world needs more light."

A Catholic Approves of Pill RU 486
January 21, 2016

How life, experience and learning can change one's opinions. Today I am hailing the approval of the early-abortion pill RU-486, recently approved, after two and a half years of study by Health Canada.

This pill will induce a medical abortion, doing away with the need for a surgical and more complicated one.

But in the sixties, I actually debated the morality of abortion on Cable TV in Montreal. My opponent was Dr Henry Morgentaler. As I recall, he politely defeated me, rather roundly. My firm, even smug, "pro-life" views at the time were shaped by the fact that I was a young married woman with two small children, a loving and loyal spouse, and enough money to live on. Not single, poor and pregnant.

Moreover, I was steeped, uncritically as I know now, in the dominant Catholic teaching on sex and reproduction. I knew nothing of the longstanding minority Catholic position that exists on these matters.

So I might have been a touch arrogant, convinced of his ethical inferiority. After all, he was a slightly suspicious immigrant doctor who actually had clinics for women seeking abortions, and he was public about it.

The story of the next 20 years shows that Dr Morgentaler, who is a member of the Order of Canada, advocated for women and choice at immense personal cost, spending many months in jail. Then in 1988, the Supreme Court of Canada led by Justices Bertha Wilson and Brian Dickson, ruled that the state has no business in the private medical decisions of a woman, and it struck down any restrictions.

Unevenly, with much struggle, access to surgical abortion has advanced across the country, with only PEI not providing services today. More good news is that abortion numbers have been going down in Canada, to under 90,000 a year.

Maybe that is due to improved sex education and contraception, and the rise of women as assertive moral agents.

The issue has been bitterly divisive. Sadly, the "pro-life" lobby has been led, I'd suggest, by badly informed evangelicals and Catholics. Today, *Campaign Life*, funded partly by the Knights of Columbus, organizes a March for Life every May on Parliament Hill. Regrettably, Catholic school boards, which are publicly funded and should not be propagandizing youth, bring busloads of students to the rally.

Campaign Life distributed ugly pamphlets showing candidate Justin Trudeau and aborted fetuses last fall. Now Prime Minister, a Catholic and father of three, Trudeau requires all Liberal candidates to be "pro-choice." In all this political rhetoric, the unhappily pregnant woman is rarely considered. She has been humiliated, demonized and denounced. Yet France has had RU 486 for 25 years, America for 15.

As Heather Mallick writes in the Toronto Star, "For teenagers, frightened wives and girlfriends, and those with punitive families, it is a more private way to make this central and personal decision."

This series of two pills will induce an abortion process much like a miscarriage. A woman may at last have the privacy that will shield her from harassment. Expected to be available in the spring, mifegymiso will be prescribed and supervised by a doctor over a period of two weeks. It is intended for early stages of pregnancy, up to 49 days.

And we can all get back to educating ourselves and others about respect for conscience, about responsibility in relationships, and about recognizing sexual violence. We may learn about disagreeing civilly.

And the Catholic thing? Well, Canon Law, always in revision, was last updated in 1983. Canon 1398 still excommunicates anyone who procures or performs an abortion.

Excommunication itself is badly understood and certainly is not explained in our parishes. It is a temporary ban from the sacraments. It does not apply to those like me who advocate for choice.

In fact, two great theologians, Thomas Aquinas and Augustine did not consider the fetus in the early stages to be a person. There is another primary Catholic moral principle: one's conscience is not to be violated.

We Read, We Really Read
January 28, 2016

If there is in Peterborough a location more inviting, more inclusive and more democratic than the Public Library, I don't know what it is.

I am a heavy library user. Sometimes for a one-on-one session, which is free on modern technology, sometimes picking up a book I've requested online, having been alerted on email that it awaits me, sometimes using using the website *Overdrive* to download a book to my iPad from the Ontario Library Service.

Then again I browse the CDs in the library, which have a reasonable one-week borrowing time, or have a cup of coffee, or glance through newspapers. In fact, for the unloved task of grading student English papers of which I have a few every year, I leave my kitchen table and go to the library, to a desk, where the slight formality there keeps me on task. No housekeeping distractions.

I see the ordinary folks of our city, those without computers at all, at work in the section of free computers. That sure helps bridge the digital divide: a computer with a word processing function and internet access.

I see some people just in out of the cold. I can book the downstairs auditorium for public meetings at a reasonable rate. I can even put books I am giving away into the chute at the back of the building. There is a Tuesday afternoon Book Club for interested people. At it, newcomers can meet like-minded readers. Sometimes, when I ask, a diligent librarian will find a book I seek on Interlibrary loan. I think they are skilled detectives of information.

I watch from a distance as the children's librarians encourage, guide and delight children. A recent study found that citizens in Ontario value two municipal services above all others: the fire service and the library. Above police and snow removal and rinks!

There are 1200 visitors every day to the library. It has 55,000 members with cards and of these 27,000 are active. Now that's a large number of users.

Some more numbers: there are 51 employees of the library, 16 fulltime and 35 part-time. It is open 59 hours a week. Most of us would like to see it open longer hours, particularly earlier in the morning. To its credit, the library seeks public comment and posts the messages it gets, along with replies.

I chatted last week with Adam Coones, a 14-year employee, now assistant clerical supervisor and representative for library workers on CUPE. What's to happen to our library now? The main branch will move temporarily to Peterborough Square in April. It may be there for 14 months, until a planned renovation is completed that will cost $12 million, funds coming mostly from the City. Thirty dollars of our property taxes go each year to the library budget. Seventy percent of the collection will move to the Square too. The architectural firm designing the renovation is VG Architects of Toronto, who specialize in renovating educational and cultural facilities. I've looked at their website, at some of their really fine jobs.

The present library on Aylmer Street moved there in 1980, from the old site the Carnegie Building on George Street, which now houses City departments. It has become a bit shabby: heavy use will do that.

Forward-thinking library planners will be incorporating an expanded Arabic section, in light of our growing refugee population. And there is the challenge of ever-changing technology. Don't I know it. Bring on a course on FITBIT.

As I hail our library and wish it well, in the temporary location and then in the renovated space, I am convinced we actually are a bookish people. Our kids follow two tracks, the print and the digital. Information which we culled at considerable time and effort from encyclopedias, they find in a flash on Wikipedia. What's not to like about that?

But for the wisdom to sort and judge, to value and to reject material, then cultural learning and wise mentors are still crucial.

"BIG" ~ An Idea Whose Time Has Come February 4, 2016

February is a month of intense learning opportunities here in Peterborough.

No sooner has Reframe Film Festival concluded its eleventh annual weekend of global consciousness-raising documentaries (and we Canadians love our documentaries), than has come an intense, renewed look at poverty's effects on Peterborough. The movement is spreading.

A coalition of groups has come together because of their deepening concern about food insecurity in our city. Food bank use is up, good nutrition is becoming hard to afford, kids' health is at risk.

The Ontario Public Interest Research Group (OPIRG) headquartered at the university, the YWCA, Green-Up and the Health Unit are working to inform the community about this modern blight.

Called NOURISH, they work to mobilize public opinion and develop the political will towards change: change in the systems and change for individual lives.

Studying the interconnectedness of deprivations people here are suffering: not enough food, no safe and secure home, limited opportunities to develop and engage in civil society, mental illness, stress, and poor health, NOURISH realized that one feature determines one's quality of life: inadequate income.

Simple as that.

So the theory goes: let's provide a citizen's income, a regular payment of money given unconditionally by government to individuals, in addition to any income received from elsewhere.

While startling to many, it is not a new idea. In 1795, Thomas Paine, a founding father in the USA, proposed a "capital grant at the age of majority."

Social security is embedded in Canadian society, but today it is in the form of multiple programs of targeted assistance and complex mechanisms of administration, a dizzying array.

So NOURISH has a joined the Basic Income Movement, locally and across the country. Basic Income Peterborough Network, co-chaired by Susan Hubay and Jason Hartwick, is making presentations all over town and getting people talking. They call for a basic income guarantee ("BIG"), to replace our patchwork system of benefits.

Amazingly, support for the idea comes from both ends of the political spectrum. For the right wing, it has the appeal of lowering the overall costs of our means-tested social welfare benefits. For the left-wing, "BIG" advances equality and security.

All the aspects of it need airing. Councilor Henry Clarke said recently that City Council had received a request from Kingston to endorse the notion of "BIG."

Clarke said honestly, "I just don't know enough about it."

That's where most of us are.

So many angles, such as incentives and disincentives to work, and the amount of "BIG" payments across the country will need to be examined. I can envision a lively Town Hall meeting, such as we have experienced recently, facilitated by the talented Peter Pula, Ben Wolfe, Cheryl Lyon and Jocasta Boone.

As luck would have it, there are two free public meetings this month. On February 9, the eminent economist, Evelyn Forget of the University of Manitoba, will be speaking on "The Town With No Poverty" in the public meeting room of the new Health Unit on King Street at 7 pm. Forget found some good outcomes when she looked at a form of "BIG" in Dauphin, MB in the seventies: higher graduation rates, better health outcomes and less crime.

On February 22, the University Women's Club will hold an open forum at Northminster Church on the same topic.

Says Evan Brockest of NOURISH, "Peterborough is rich in two things: social capital, which is the talent and good will of its people, and a beautiful natural environment. It is poor in many ways too: 12 percent are food insecure, and we are number six in unemployment. Many people are excluded from participating in society."

We can be a pilot site for a form of "BIG," and watch our community strengthen.

Reshaping The Way We Vote
February 11, 2016

We can't postpone it any longer. We have to try to get our heads around the idea of changes/reforms to our way of voting for federal politicians. It's coming, a big national debate, and we have a special responsibility to compose some recommendations for the powers-that-be.

After all, we are Peterburians, keenly interested in a good society and in politics. We voted in healthy numbers, 74.5%, on October 19 last, and we have an MP who is leading the charge on this file.

It is therefore, as they say, incumbent on us to study up, do some hard thinking and come to a position. Or more than one position, since 80 democratic countries have some form of representation that is different from ours. On the other hand, 57 countries have the same as ours.

Our interest and enthusiasm? High. We are an alert gang, as shown by our turnout at the polls in October. We were bested only by the voters of Ottawa Centre, who voted at 75% turnout. And after all, that riding is full of civil servants. Pros.

We in Peterborough-Kawartha fretted for a long time, but then we pulled ourselves together and turfed out the party that had ruled for nine years and had provided us with a disgraced MP and a lame-duck year of no representation at all. Then we amazed ourselves that we put in a bright young immigrant woman of the Muslim faith.

We were right, again! The Prime Minister agreed with Peterborough-Kawartha, and made her Minister for Democratic Institutions.

So can we find a way to understand the choices here and give her our advice?

Change will be a daunting task, unless Parliament, which has the power to do so, decides on a certain change and legislates it. Maybe we need to go easy for a while. Some simple reforms could be tried for an election (next one: 2019) without any nation-wide vote. Here, I am indebted to the ideas of longtime political analyst Jeff Sallot.

He writes, "If we were to create Canada from scratch, we would never have an unelected Senate. A British monarch would not be our head of state. PEI would never be a province on its own. We would erase provincial boundaries and deliver health and education nationally. We would provide every citizen with a guaranteed income."

Since that nirvana will not be in place any time soon, Sallot recommends six "could do's" right away. They are: give a tax credit for voting, lower the voting age to 16, use electronic voting, call on Elections Canada to organize leaders' debates, allow free votes in the House for all election reform proposals, and then he says (somewhat vaguely), try some form of proportional representation.

I need to hear more. My next column will look at the 3 main systems being talked about.

One is the present one "First Past the Post" (FPTP). Its formal name is "single-member plurality" and it has been in effect since Confederation. We haven't done badly by any standard with it. But it delivers 100% of power to a Party with 39% of the vote. There is disaffection and disengagement in public life and in elections, I think we can all agree. And many voters (600,000 Greens for example) feel shut out, with that many votes and only one member in Canada's Parliament.

This is why we are looking at this change thing at all. After almost 150 years (in 2017), we can consider ourselves a mature democracy. We really should take a critical look at our system of elections, and examine the forms which other democracies use.

It's going to take a steady nerve and a whole lot of listening to each other.

Silence in a Wordy World
February 18, 2016

We Canadians know something about winter landscapes. We are formed by ice and snow. Weather is our favorite conversation topic.

So when I am plunged into a vastly different landscape, a desert one, I am very unbalanced for a while.

Then I strive to find an even keel, a psychological one, and start to see the beauties, the challenges and the mysteries of the new place. Every couple of years, I try to find a really quiet place to retreat to. I know it's a luxury, and most harried people can't manage it time-wise, money-wise and responsibilities-wise.

But I found myself last week at a retreat house in the Sonoran desert just north of Tucson, Arizona. A long way from home and from Peterborough in February.

My brother Brian, who is from Dryden, lives down here. He sent me a ticket and told me about this meditative centre, Roman Catholic in flavor, monastic in practice, founded in 1974, that welcomes people drawn to silence.

The Desert House of Prayer embraces complete silence except for the supper meal. About 25 people from all over the world are here: Catholics, Jews, Protestants and Buddhists, all with a long history of seeking meaning.

The theme of DHOP is "seeing flowers in the desert." That sounds like something I'd like to explore, given our modern context: noise, dire predictions for the future, and painful awareness of suffering, human and planetary.

Deserts are those pieces of land marked by very high temperatures and low precipitation.

51

America has three giant ones. Canada, by the way, has one small desert, near Kamloops, BC. My desert here has an annual rainfall of fewer than eight inches. By contrast, Toronto has 32 inches of rain each year, and 48 of snow!

We are right alongside the Saguaro National Forest. Hiking through scrub under a wide sky is unforgettable. There is a walking stick in each room.

You have to love cacti to enjoy life here. The saguaro can grow to 15 feet in height and live 200 years. It is the granddaddy of 70 types of cacti, a brave species, which includes the hedgehog, the fishhook, the prickly pear and the cholla, which is accused of jumping out at you.

In this spare, arid and even forbidding landscape, with meditation sessions three times a day, a vegetarian menu and a labyrinth pattern outlined in stones to walk in, while at the same time surrounded by books, contemporary magazines, fine classical music and even WiFi, what does one take away? Some peace of soul, for sure.

And an admiration for adaptation to circumstance. Desert flowers, some as small as one quarter of an inch, are called "belly flowers" because that's what you have to do to see them. They remain in the ground as seeds until conditions are favorable, and then they germinate like mad. They conserve every drop of water, curling their leaves inward, growing special roots and opening their pores only at night.

The birds: a gila woodpecker taps into the giant cactus, a mourning dove keens a lament, the cactus wren is a real cutie. Lizards and the occasional coyote and javelina. Horses and riders clip clop along the washes, under three ragged, brown mountain ranges. I make it part way up Sombrero Peak, and find Box Canyon.

It all dislocates a person from the north and at the same time opens one to new thoughts. Rabbi Michael Lerner says "Silence is Sabbath, including rest, pleasure, freedom and slowness."

Naturally I'm reading the sayings of the desert mothers and a few of the desert fathers too. These hardy folks fled Egyptian and Syrian towns in the fourth century, some 40,000 men and women, to reject the values of the Roman Empire and to seek ultimate meaning. They left some writings.

Now that's a long way back, but I'm not one of those who thinks the ancients have nothing to say to the modern mind. We need all the help we can get.

Fit-Bitting Along
February 25, 2016

When it comes to the use of technology, I'm probably somewhere in the middle. It's been a quick and complete revolution in communication for my demographic, the over-sixties, and we have had to be nimble.

And humble. Used to answering questions for a long time, we now have to ask them. Of twelve-year-olds.

But we love the communication it enables. We just have to get it under our control, and set limits and deal with anxiety. There have been losses and gains.

I use email but check it just once a day. I pay bills online but like to receive hard-copy-in-the-mailbox invoices. I have a cell phone, on the cheapest possible plan, for emergency calls and for texting. One son responds immediately to texts, and nothing else. I don't think it's a Smartphone I have. No need for that. I watch younger people type on those small keyboards and am amazed at their dexterity and speed.

At a gathering of Peterborough sponsors and a Syrian family who speak no English, I saw the proficiency with which the Canadians used their phones and a translation application to show Arabic phrases to their guests.

I have a land-line with caller-identity, since we are still subjected to junk calls in spite of having registered not to get them. My land-line has an answering machine. My television is now a thin one (HD, I think it's called) and therefore the sound is less satisfying than it was with the fat one. I have learned to pre-record and playback, but I mostly watch network television. For really difficult questions, such as "How do I stream something?" Des from next door comes over.

My newspaper is still delivered in hard copy every day. Good visceral experience, reading with paper in hand and coffee nearby. I send these columns to *The Examiner* by email. Do you know my editor, poor man, receives 1000 emails a day? Have a heart.

I use Facebook, and probably post too many political stories. At least my sister says I do, and she has blocked me.

Just think, in 20 years, what electricity and Steve Jobs and Mark Zuckerberg have enabled. Do we really understand the changes in our society, our psychology and our very physical selves? Are sociologists catching up with these questions?

Then there is the need to monitor the hours we spend on the devices. Some people set alarms to go off after an hour; other families have a box in which to place devices as people gather for a meal. Some teachers say, "Shut down everything! We look each other in the eye in this class."

Into my life has come "wearable technology." Family members took up a collection and gave me a Fitbit for Christmas. One of them "synched" it to my computer, and now the information I get on myself is astounding. Narcissism, anyone? I learn all about my steps taken, kilometres walked, calories burned, sleep patterns and steps climbed. The bionic woman, without incisions.

The Fitbit does motivate me to walk. It's a good day when I can leave the car in the driveway anyway.

I now notice Fitbits on other people. By the way, one can make friends with Fitbitters and follow their progress. The competition does not excite me. However, I do enjoy the congratulatory beeps and whistles my Fitbit makes when I have made 10,000 steps in a day.

It seems in modern life we are always running to catch up with what has just happened. Change comes very speedily. Out there are thousands of self-described geeks and nerds bent over their computers designing the next great technological thing.

My job will be to say open-minded as to its benefits and drawbacks; its nuisance value versus its cost; its role in fostering inclusion or exclusion, in promoting health or impairment, and in using resources.

Human Rights for All:
the Peterborough Effort
March 3, 2016

There's a small group of people in town that amazes me year after year with their calm in the face of painful, often awful, knowledge of crimes and inhumanity.

It is Amnesty International Group 46, now 32 years old.

In 1961 in Britain, a lawyer, Peter Benenson, became enraged when he read a story about two Portuguese students being imprisoned for raising a toast to freedom. He wrote a newspaper article and coined the phrase "prisoners of conscience." The response all over Europe was immediate. Amnesty International was born, and in the years following has become a leading research institute investigating and publicizing abuse of human rights anywhere in the world. Then it organizes actions on behalf of victims.

Amnesty works on cases of abuse, torture, disappearances and other injustices, both in Canada and elsewhere, in a pro-active but peaceful way. It depends heavily on grassroots small groups, both for fundraising and for activism.

The Peterborough group meets monthly, has about 15 members and dozens of supporters. Amnesty in Canada has two branches: Anglophone, headed by the impressive Alex Neve, a New Brunswicker, and Francophone, headed by Beatrice Vaugrante. A very effective pair.

The small group here carries on year after year. They maintain good humour and a clear-headedness as they tackle the next outrage. This seems to me to mark a deeply nourished spiritual self, a great maturity, and courage to face both dismissal and criticism.

They seek to know what's going on in the world: to be informed about man's inhumanity to man everywhere. They believe that knowing is better than not knowing. But it's not enough to rest there, with knowledge. Acting, that's the key.

The act may be small, slight: a letter written, an opinion formed, a remark made where people are listening or a new attitude assumed. There is enormous evidence that in the world, cruelty happens again and again. But it is not the final answer. The AI watchword seems to be taken from American Rabbi Rami Shapiro: "You are not obligated to complete the work of relieving the world's grief. But neither are you free to abandon it."

Abandon? Ask Connie Parry, an original member 32 years ago; ask Janet Bradley, coordinator for 15; ask Daphne Ingram, whose prodigious energy brings us Reframe Film Festival, Canadian Women for Women of Afghanistan and Amnesty Group 46, Peterborough. Or ask Alan Dunne, who alerts the group to urgent action cases where an individual's very life is at stake.

Just recently, we heard that, with Russian support, the Syrian regime had bombed hospitals and children's centres in the north of the country. What could be more horrifying?

But these AI folks just got back to work, documenting, informing protesting, writing letters and raising awareness, urging governments and the UN to say something: to examine where their arms are sold, and to ask where funding comes from for such atrocities.

Group 46's annual dinner which had an Indigenous theme, just raised about $1000 to be sent to Ottawa for Amnesty Canada work. A.I. Canada has 75,000 members and an annual budget of 11 million dollars. Not a cent from government or from corporations.

There have been resounding successes this year: Omar Khadr was released on bail in Alberta; many Mexican prisoners of conscience were released, and one, Angel Colon, a human rights defender, came to Canada and said, "My freedom is your victory." Pressure is building to have Canada sign and ratify the document banning torture worldwide. A national inquiry into missing and murdered aboriginal girls and women has been called. Shell Oil cleaned up an oil spill in Niger. Ireland became the first country in the world to declare full civil marriage equality. Mohammed Fahmy, a journalist, was freed in Egypt. Raif Badawi in Saudi Arabia, who is jailed for blogging against the government has been spared the series of lashes first imposed. And the Liberal government is listening and involved.

A little success keeps Group 46 going.

"Trumpery at Work" or *"Another Day, Another Outrage"* *March 10, 2016*

No self-respecting columnist can put off forever writing about the dominant American phenomenon of the day: the nasty buffoon as candidate.

What are they thinking? This great republic to our south: our best neighbours, we with our shared European and global culture.

Our distinct differences in history and politics and values, are in sharp relief now.

About DT, he is an odious presence on all media: wildly self-absorbed, clueless, insulting, the unlikeable great uncle you have had to sometimes tolerate, a monster created by his careless Party.

But near the Presidency? Now that's frightening. A misogynistic demagogue who borders on fascism in his racist rants.

More even than his personality, that silly, naked greed and stupidity, is the utter failure of American public education to form critical citizens and thinkers. Who are these DT supporters? Mary Anne Mc Farlane, a Peterborough friend, told me she was in South Carolina and went to a Trump rally. She is white, so had no trouble getting in. I would go, too, if I had a chance, just to observe the crowd. She said it was chilling: fanatic, raging, irrational cries and slogans.

Even worse perhaps, is the fawning attention given DT by mainstream media people. Wolf Blitzer, Mike Wallace, Anderson Cooper, not to mention the dreadful *FOX News*, those guys who form public opinion in America, taking DT seriously, quite respectfully. They even go so far as to excuse the behaviour and remarks of DT supporters, saying, those poor Republicans feel left out, they aren't progressing financially; their country isn't what it used to be.

Have those interviewers and commentators spoken out, taken him on, read the situation and warned their viewers with some straight talking? I haven't seen it. I have all lost respect for mainstream television's ability to affect the common good. (Caveat: my Boston friend says *NPR Radio*, the *Wall Street Journal*, and the *New York Times* are highly critical of DT.) DT actually said about Malala Yousufsai, who criticized him: "I prefer Noble Laureates who haven't been shot in the head." There is no depth to which he will not sink. Don't even look up his ten worst comments about people. He has said, "I love the poorly-educated."

And the Grand Old Party (GOP), the political party of Lincoln, now with craven Republican leadership, mincing and dancing around, repelled by this man but coveting a possible election victory.

But we can be thankful for late night comics and some blogs. I recommend *www.salon.com*.

Humour has always been a saving grace. I know enlightened Americans who only get their news through the filter of satire late at night. Who could match John Oliver of *Last Week Tonight* with his hilarious 21 minute expose of trumpery, culminating in his campaign to "makeDonaldDrumpf." Thousands have signed on.

J.K. Rowling has said DT is a worse villain than Lord Voldemort. Young readers, is that true? Then there are the Facebook contributions. Somebody recently looked up "trumpery" in the dictionary. There it is: "Trumpery: from the French 'tromper,' to deceive or cheat; anything calculated to deceive by false show; externally splendid, but intrinsically of little value."

How could Webster have known in advance? That definition could describe DT's platform.

We have to endure this until November of this year. I feel sure that Hillary Clinton will win the election then. The northeast and California will have something to say about DT. But the legacy of this kind of ugly, divisive campaigning will last, and will be sobering for America to think about. Important rules of civilized public behaviour have been irreparably broken.

As someone has said, this is not Germany in 1933, and DT is not AH, but there are uncomfortable echoes in style, exploitation and scapegoating. And extreme nationalism.

Many dogs have been loosed. Not to insult dogs.

Canadians watch and ponder and sympathize and hope.

59

So Much Carbon, So Little Time
March 17, 2016

Creative and daring small groups keep coming to my attention in Peterborough.

Transition Town is one of them. Founded here in 2007 by the visionary Fred Irwin, it is kept alive by a small band of committed people, among them Cheryl Lyon, Michael Bell, Pat Remy and Trent Rhode.

"Transition Town" is an idea first enunciated by an environmentalist in England named Rob Hopkins in 2005. You might enjoy his TED talk from 2009.

Hopkins had come to the conclusion that the evidence for global warming, which would do deep harm to our planet earth, was incontrovertible. Change was coming, no matter what we did as governments and individuals and corporations. The global urgency we now feel from the 195 governments who met in Paris in December, where they pledged not to allow the temperature to rise more than 2 degrees C above that which existed before the Industrial Revolution, is much needed, and we must hold their feet to the fire, literally.

Elizabeth May said recently that an eminent climate scientist was asked about the consequences of a temperature rise of 2 degrees. "That will mean 7 or 8 feet of sea-level rise," he said; "the Greenland ice sheet will melt, as well as the Western Arctic ice sheet." Beware Florida and Bangladesh. And New York and London and Halifax.

The Liberal government of Canada set good targets in Paris, and promised a detailed plan by March 12, 2016. However, the only enforcement mechanism across the world at this point is government-to-government peer pressure.

At the very same time, another parallel task lies before us: to prepare, to adapt, to be realistic, and to reduce bad effects already launched on the world.

We must "transition" (the word has now become a verb), to low-carbon living, and at the same time strengthen local communities to absorb the shocks, and come out of it alive. Chastened but perhaps wiser. It will mean simpler living, localized eating, all the "green" habits, a co-operative attitude and an economy of local entrepreneurship.

Transition Town Peterborough is energetic and forward-thinking. Endorsed by City Council in 2008, we were the first Canadian community to declare ourselves a "transition town." TTP has introduced the Kawartha Loon, a complementary currency, issued at 10% discount by the Peterborough Community Credit Union and accepted by 100 local businesses, shops and services. Hail to Peterborough Mitsubishi and to Rocky Ridge Drinking Water for stepping up to accept the Loons. Many restaurants are on board: By the Bridge, Black Honey, Dreams of Beans, Elmhirsts, Peterborough Eats, and the Silver Bean to name a few.

As for shopping, if we could transition our food purchases to 25% local sources, we could have an overall economic impact of 400 million dollars in ten years. All here in the region.

TTP organizes the Purple Onion Festival each year on September 21, celebrating food and culture. There is Dandelion Day on May 28, encouraging illness prevention through complementary health practices, and the impressive magazine, *Greenzine*, four times a year.

Fifteen per cent of Canadians are deeply distressed by signs of earth's deterioration. They fear global economic collapse. Their mental health is suffering. Fifteen percent of Canadians, woefully, are climate deniers. The rest, mostly in the middle, are worried, but unsure what to do next. Transition Town Peterborough lets them know and increases their hope.

There are now two thousand groups in 50 countries. Each is unique: they have a shared vision but their own local projects. They are volunteer-based, active, well-informed and localized.

Rob Hopkins published a booklet which he took to Paris in 2015 outlining 21 grassroots projects from around the world. Peterborough's was included.

As science issues a steady drumbeat of alarming weather stories, stories of habitat ruination, extinct species and increasing deserts, the Transition Town movement offers leadership, involvement and intelligent behaviours to us all.

A Time of Awakening
March 24, 2016

I may be experiencing a heavy dose of wishful thinking just now, but I feel as if we are in a renaissance period of native culture, and more importantly, a new and appreciative awareness of its importance in the dominant society.

In the "Settler" society. That's us. I think we are exhibiting more curiosity, more humility, and more honoring of aboriginal wisdom.

In recent days these things have happened, and I've been there.

At Sadleir House recently, a group of fifteen teacher-trainees from Trent's education department ended their four-day course called *Teaching Outside the Box* with a powerful talk by Beedahbin Peltier, Indigenous Studies instructor-advisor at Fleming College. He told his story of growing up in Wikwemikong First Nation on Manitoulin Island, resisting school but then becoming a student, and learning wisdom from his grandfather. He said he believes Canadian society is at a crossroads and he is hopeful.

In Ottawa, Hon Carolyn Bennett, cabinet minister in charge of Indigenous issues, and a woman I know (she was one of my campers years ago at a girls' camp near Port Severn) announced that the number of aboriginal women missing and murdered is much higher than previously believed, as high as 4000. She and Justice Minister Jodie Wilson-Raybould are moving quickly to set up the inquiry as promised.

At the Unitarian worship service on Sunday, Minister Julie Stoneberg spoke eloquently about four recommendations she feels her congregation can act on, as she held up and read from the *Truth and Reconciliation Report*.

At the Elders Conference at Trent, Pegi Eyers, a white woman with a strong advocate's heart, offered her new book, *Ancient Spirit Rising: Reclaiming Your Roots & Restoring Earth Community*, a passionate plea for white transformation. The book is being widely praised in many countries.

There is widespread talk that Mr Trudeau should name as a new senator Justice Murray Sinclair, articulate chair of the Truth and Reconciliation Commission.

At the Amnesty Dinner on February 21, Indigenous women leaders Tasha Beeds and Shirley Williams led a sacred water ceremony and invited people to walk with them on May 8, as they circumnavigate Little Lake in their seventh and final "Water Walk."

The cover of the new *Greenzine* magazine has the banner: "Peterborough City, County and First Nations." Editor Cheryl Lyon consulted native leaders and received their permission to put "First Nations" on the magazine cover.

Most delightful of all is the exhibit now mounted at the Art Gallery of Peterborough, celebrating the glowing and magnificent paintings, 45 in all, by Arthur Shilling, a member of Mnjikaning First Nation near Orillia. It is a stunning exhibit which will be at the Gallery until May 22.

Our gallery is free and open Tuesday through Sunday, 11-5 pm. Educator Jane Wild is receiving calls from teachers setting up visits from students of all ages. She offers two-hour sessions, including a tour and a painting session, all supplies provided.

A brilliantly gifted artist, Shilling painted a prodigious number of works featuring faces, his own and that of his wife and sons, and many aboriginal people. Shilling died in 1986, only 45 years of age. He felt an urgency to create as many canvases as he could, knowing his limited lifespan.

They make up a national treasure. Pain and resilience, vivid colour, confident brush strokes, altogether an unforgettable experience of art.

Friend Willam Kingfisher has spent three years assembling the collection, the first ever, negotiating with individuals and galleries who own the paintings. One woman told him she had great trouble parting with her Shilling work, even for two years. There is a 30-foot mural in four panels, with some empty space left for the future work in the last panel.

Kingfisher pays tribute to the initiative of the AGP in bringing forward the idea of this exhibit and finding the financing for it. Not to be missed.

Voting Systems 101
March 31, 2016

Many people find our present system of electing a federal government easy to understand. It is the only one we've ever known. It is the "FPTP" (First Past the Post) method, officially known as "Single Member Plurality."

But at the same time, many other people are puzzled that one party wins a majority government without a majority of the votes. That's the situation we are in today. Seven million Canadians may be thinking they cast "wasted" votes in the last election because we operated under FPTP.

To recap, FPTP has been in place since the 12th century. We have been getting one ballot and voting for one candidate whose party affiliation we know, in one specific geographic area. Its supporters say it provides strong and effective government because its bills come to the legislature with a good chance of being passed.

But its weaknesses loom large too. There is a lack of fairness to other voters who have been shut out, and an exclusion of political points of view. There is no incentive to make deals with other parties.

Co-operation tends to be less, and hostility tends to be greater. I know teachers who value civility who are appalled to take kids to see their Parliament.

So now we are into a period of study and debate about voting. Many folks, some of my family, just glaze over and change the subject.

Others are impassioned advocates for change. Many civic leaders: David Suzuki, Maude Barlow, Hugh Segal, Stephane Dion and Elizabeth May among them, are lobbying for some form of Proportional Representation.

The Liberal government says that we will have change by election 2019. I confess I'm struggling to understand the choices before us. I consult voting systems guru Wilf Day in Port Hope. He does his best with me.

Proportional representation is any voting system where the number of seats won by a party is proportional to the number of votes received. If a party gets 30% of the vote, they get 30% of the seats. All votes cast, therefore, contribute to the results.

Let's start with Proportional IDEA #1: the single transferable vote, STV. That's the one recommended by B.C.'s Citizens' Assembly in 2004, and voted on twice. It didn't get accepted out there because it didn't receive the required 60% support from the people.

STV, as do other PR systems, requires the use of multi-member voting districts. For example, an enlarged Peterborough-Kawartha riding would have several MPs! The House of Commons total would still be 338 MPs, so the ridings would have to be bigger.

Present boundaries of ridings would be changed, enlarged. A non-partisan Boundaries Commission is proposed for setup in 2017, and we will have their recommendations in place by Feb 2019, leaving 7 months before the next federal election.

Furthermore, the proportionality part kicks in after the polls close and formulas are applied.

Some of us ain't going to like that. We like the cut-and-thrust of election night, Peter Mansbridge, breathless predictions and coloured charts.

The formula to be applied goes like this. Let's say our riding can elect 3 persons. The quota part kicks in and it's figured out this way.

Take the total number of ballots cast (10,000). Take the total number of candidates to be elected (3). Add one more to the total of candidates (now 4). Divide the total votes cast by the number of people to be elected, plus one. That's 10,000 divided by 4. Let me get my calculator here; it's 2500.

So if Maggie Muggins gets 2500 or more, she's elected. Her surplus votes, over the 2500, are now distributed among the other candidates according to voters' second choice indicators. If James Bond gets to 2500 with these surplus votes, he's elected. The lowest candidate drops off: her votes are redistributed, and so on, till we have 3 elected candidates. Like it?

Now, Einstein, let's take a break.

My final column on this matter will be soon: the Mixed Member Proportional (MMP) system.

"The Pitmen Painters" Honours Miners April 7, 2016

I am the proud daughter of a mining town: Kirkland Lake.

My first 18 years were spent growing up in the mostly poor, gold-mining community, living through boom and bust periods of relative prosperity and risk, when gold was selling at $35 an ounce. (Now it's $1235). When I lived there, the population was 25,000 people. Today it is 8500.

66

It was for the miners, hardscrabble and dangerous work, done in the thirties and forties and fifties by mostly immigrant Italians and Poles, and the mid-level professionals who served them. All the while developing hockey players!

In 1994, at long last, a striking Miners Memorial, remembering the 100 or more miners who have died in mining accidents in Kirkland Lake's seven mines in the 20th century, was erected at the gateway of the town. Schooling there at Kirkland Lake Collegiate and Vocational Institute gave me an inclusive general education in a fairly humble setting, with flashes of inspiration from some teachers, and a glimpse that life could offer more learning. Culture and its richness was not the reserve of the well-to-do.

So I have a kind of visceral reaction to mining communities. With added sympathy and understanding of the theme, I recently watched a moving rehearsal of the new play *The Pitmen Painters*, in an empty George Street office space. It will open Friday, April 8 at Market Hall for a run of six performances.

Written in 2007 by the talented British playwright Lee Hall, who gained fame and admiration by writing *Billy Elliot* which was about the working-class son of British family who aspires to be a dancer, *The Pitmen Painters* explores a profound human truth: no matter the class and background, the human person strives to know more, to be more and to understand more.

Following the true story of a group of coal miners from the rough-and-tumble area of Newcastle, England in the forties, *The Pitmen Painters* renders a winning portrait of five miners who undertake an art appreciation course, offered at their local union hall.

Riotously funny, the adult students first off quarrel amongst themselves, then utter their first words of misapprehension as they gaze on famous paintings, and also register their shock as a young woman who arrives to be their model for life drawing begins to disrobe.

Their patient tutor does not patronize them but continues to offer opportunities to visit galleries and encourages them to think and to paint. They slowly become known and respected in the art world as "The Ashington Group."

The indefatigable artist-producer Randy Read, a consummate casting director who is committed to Peterborough, is mounting the play here starting April 8. Read, who was inducted into the Peterborough Pathway of Fame in 2011, was born in Peterborough, grew up in Mount Pleasant and attended Crestwood Secondary School and Trent University. He founded New Stages Theatre Company 20 years ago and has enriched life here with his yearly series of three staged readings, mostly new and contemporary plays featuring nationally-known Canadian actors. New Stages Reading Series started in, and then outgrew Showplace Lounge and is now at Market Hall.

Read believes art is of crucial importance in engaging the heart and mind. He first read *The Pitmen Painters* in 2013, and determined to bring it to Peterborough. He has assembled experienced equity actors who live in the Peterborough region. Obviously relishing their roles in an important play, Robert Ainsworth, Brad Brackenridge, Edward Charette, Kait Dueck, Dianne Latchford, Tim Walker, Mark Wallace and Robert Winslow move the audience with their deep grasp of the characters, their dilemmas and their growth.

I can think of no more enriching experience for everybody. In our age of screens and filters, there is still the reality that live, competent storytelling is the best.

www.newstages.ca

A Look at Mixed-Member Proportional (MMP)
April 14, 2016

Are you willing to plunge into this topic one more time? The voting system called MMP is about to be unpacked: Mixed-Member Proportional.

Fair Vote Canada, the national non-partisan advocacy group which lobbies for proportional representation (any variety), does not endorse one or other of the systems before us. They are trying to do a massive education job and recently created an alliance called Every Voter Counts.

Among the members of the alliance are the YWCA, the Broadbent Institute, the Council of Canadians, Idle No More, the Canadian Labour Congress, Lead-now, Democracy Watch, the Council of Agencies Serving Immigrants, and some important thinkers: Alex Himelfarb, former Clerk of the Privy Council, Col Pat Stogran, the veterans' advocate, Stephane Dion, present Minister for Global Affairs, and none other than Guy Giorno, who was Stephen Harper's Chief of Staff.

Their study of 3000 Canadians has shown that 70% of us want a change, a stronger democracy, but we are now in a time crunch. A parliamentary committee, soon to be named, will study the options and recommend a system. Then, in about a year, debate will take place and legislation passed, and Elections Canada will move into high gear to make it work for election 2019.

One of the big tasks will be to re-draw boundaries so that we will be voting for local members (two-thirds of the House of Commons) and for regional members (one-third of the House). Total seats remain the same: 338. Therefore, the size of ridings will increase.

In MMP, we will get two ballots. Then, we can vote for a person and for a party, maybe different from each other. Two thirds of the 338 members (207 people) will be elected as local MP's, just as now.

The final one-third of MP's (131 people) will be elected from one of a newly created set of 27 regions. A region would include several (9 -11) ridings. The regional candidates could be from an "open" or a "closed" list.

How such lists are formed is a sticky question, because the political parties play the important role in developing them. But one experienced commentator says that the lists have actually included more diversity, and more youth and women than the local slate.

Lest we flinch at the newness of all this, let's remember that 87% of OECD countries use some form of proportional representation. Germany, Scotland and New Zealand use MMP. Turnout of voters in PR countries has been shown to be higher. We in Canada aren't doing well in turnouts. In the 1990's, Canada ranked 109th in the world in voter turnout, tied with Benin and just behind Lebanon. Yikes.

The U.S. and the UK do not have P.R., but let's not be too influenced by their process. Let's talk and choose a "made in Canada" system, taking into account our great wide geography, our uneven population clusters and our regional differences.

As it is now, with FPTP, it's just not fair, and we Canadians have a demonstrated commitment to fairness. For example, with the vote share they won in 2015, the Green Party would now have 10 members in the House of Commons. Right now they have one. We'd benefit from more Greens.

What I figure, is that finally, if we Canadians can adopt Smartphones and electric cars and robots, we can get our heads around election changes for 2019. We won't each get all our favorite features, but we will in the end have a much more representative system of electing our decision-makers. Then, one hopes, a lot more younger voters will engage, who believe that all sides will be heard, including theirs. Let's get closer to a country that represents everyone. One of my most trusted advisors, a young father of three, says: "The two crucial issues for me are climate change and democratic reform."

Let's get on with them.

Going Global at Trent
April 21, 2016

It is a great thing to live in an university town. I first came to Peterborough in 1969, and Trent had been founded just five years earlier.

In many subtle and profound ways, it has shaped life here. I occasionally pick up a copy of *Arthur*, the student newspaper. The "Arthur" reference calls to mind all things Camelot, the medieval King Arthur and his Knights, and the vivid Trent symbol of a great sword, Excalibur, plunged into a lake as per the legend.

A few weeks ago, the newspaper *Arthur* told me about a one-evening course for five dollars, in Russian cooking, out at a Trent café called The Seasoned Spoon. You know, perogies and borscht. That would be fun, I thought. I have long nurtured an interest in all things Russian.

So I met Anna and Dariya, the enthusiastic cook-teachers and members of the 30-person Trent Russian-Speaking Club. They then came over to lunch, taught me a few Russian phrases and even put in a text call to dad in Russia to ask him exactly what books I might read to get a better grasp of Russian history and culture. Just another simple, friendly Peterborough exchange.

It reminded me to look in on Trent's International Program office and see what that great enterprise in global education, started in 1982 by first president Thomas Symons, then-Dean Robert Campbell and the late Jack Mathews, had become.

Michael Allcott, warm and thoughtful, has been director of TIP for 13 years.

The TIP motto is: "TIP believes that every Trent student should have the opportunity to develop his or her global citizenship by living, learning and making lasting friendships with people from all over the world."

There is a mutuality to this self-understanding in TIP. The department, which also facilitates 150 Trent students studying abroad any given year, believes that everyone benefits.

The numbers are astonishing. This year, over 500 undergraduate students have come from 80 countries around the world to study at Trent. They are joined by 150 more who are here for intensive English-language training prior to post-secondary enrolment, and another 75 in graduate studies.

The TIP office is centrally located in Champlain College and has six employees in addition to the Director. It is a big job: integrating and counselling these overseas students, with such activities as a four-day orientation camp in September, cultural showcases, helping them troubleshoot in a new society, fostering regional groupings such as the Russian, Chinese, South Asian and Latin American student associations, and linking with the Peterborough community.

And the financing? It used to be that the Canadian International Development Agency provided a lot of scholarships to worthy students from mostly developing countries. CIDA ended this support in 1992. Since then, Trent has led Canada in providing scholarships to international students, but now there are just 15 full scholarships. So the clientele is more middle-class and well-to-do, paying its way, which is three times the cost of that for Canadian students. But still, 22% of international students get some form of financial assistance. And as an "industry" international education offered in Canada is a huge economic boon. It outstrips mining and forestry as a foreign exchange earner. And it brings talent.

The best part for Allcott is that almost every international student reports to him experiences of warm welcome and friendly inclusion from Peterborough people. The New Canadians Centre, the Kawartha World Issues Centre, and OPIRG are just some of the local agencies which benefit. The ordinary Peterborough citizen, even casually, becomes more accustomed to a constantly-evolving Canadian society, and participates in a shrinking world.

And as for Anna, my Russian friend, she was recently elected to the Student Council at Trent. She is Vice President with responsibility for University and College Affairs.

To LEAP Or Not
April 28, 2016

I just re-read the LEAP manifesto. (*www.leapmanifesto.org*) It has been getting a lot of press, negative attention and discussion for three weeks. Actually intended for all Canadians and all political parties, it was (probably mistakenly) launched at the NDP national convention in Edmonton three weeks ago.

That convention was already heavy with drama: the political fate of Thomas Mulcair.

LEAP is a very short, four-page composition with lots of headings, white space and directness. I've read editorials and student essays longer. So it is accessible to all. Interested persons might want to consult it firsthand. And then join the great national debate.

I looked up the word "manifesto." It is a "published verbal declaration of the intentions, motives and views of the issuer, whether an individual, group, political party or government."

LEAP is ringing, sincere, passionate and, I think, full of unassailable truths. A brilliant climate scientist I know has recommended I subscribe to an environmental newsletter called *The Daily Digest* on email. In it, brief stories from around the world about our worsening climate situation keep me feeling urgently concerned, even as I bask in life in the Kawarthas: no coastal floods, no zika virus, no drought, no earthquakes.

LEAP was written by a committee of well-informed Canadians. Just check the list.

And launched right during a federal election campaign, when it wasn't at all certain that we would turn out the sitting government, which had such a dismal record on environmental issues.

Last September, when I read about the meeting in Toronto of respected groups and leading Canadians, I read the statement and signed on. So did 38,000 other Canadians.

It had the ring of urgency, a kind of biblical passion and a deep concern for the common good. LEAP starts out in no uncertain terms: "Our record on climate change is a crime against humanity's future."

It calls for no new infrastructure projects (that means pipelines) which are aimed at increasing extraction. It calls for an end to trade deals that hinder our efforts to rebuild local economies and regulate corporations. And an absolute end to fracking.

It insists on adherence to previously-stated values: respect for Indigenous rights, internationalism, human rights, diversity and environmental stewardship. It calls for green jobs, not for putting people out of work.

LEAP proclaims: "Caring for one another and caring for the planet could be the economy's fastest-growing sectors."

The time is short, which is why we need to "leap." Researchers at Stanford University have drawn up a scenario that shows Canada can transition to renewables: solar, wind, geothermal, hydro-electric and tidal turbine in 20 years.

LEAP wants retraining for workers in carbon-intensive jobs, ensuring they are able to fully participate in the clean-energy economy. It does not call for an immediate end to fossil fuel production in Canada. Nor for anyone to be thrown out of work. Fear-mongers among our pundits are getting it wrong. The NDP called it a statement of principle, which it is, and for concentrated study and response across the country.

Sympathize with Alberta premier Rachel Notley, in a province where 70,000 jobs have been lost because of the worldwide glut of oil and falling prices. In a bit of a panic she called LEAP "thoughtless, naïve and tone-deaf." She is the one facing the implications of a fossil-free economy and a huge dislocation in Alberta. This is where the rubber of noble thought and vision meets the gritty road of political implementation.

Strategically and in retrospect, it is probable that LEAP should have been launched in another forum so that it would not have been so readily dismissed as partisan NDP policy. So be it. It is out there for us now, and it is capable of inspiring. Maybe we need both grand calls and pragmatic plans. Ethics and action. A profound and ongoing national debate.

This is the LEAP which will matter.

Time to Talk Death and Dying in Canada May 5, 2016

This will be the first of two articles, today and on May 12, initiating a discussion on Bill C-14, the "Medical Assistance in Dying" act currently before Parliament and expected to be passed by June 6.

It seems as if every week we newly-aroused Canadians are asked to consider another serious moral, ethical and even religious issue that requires attention.

Attention, because our legislators are moving towards change. Many big issues face us right now: election reform and curbing carbon emissions are just two. None is easy and all need civil debate and amended laws.

But for me, the dominant question pressing in on us is that of assisted dying. The government of Canada has just tabled a bill in the House called C-14 and it must be passed, amended or not, by June 6. That gives us 6 weeks.

One commentator called it "a tectonic shift in medicine." The Vice-President of the Canadian Medical Association, Dr Jeff Blackmer said, "It is the first time in centuries the medical profession is being asked to take on a completely new role and it will take time." But the CMA is in favour of the changes.

The Canadian public has indicated in poll after poll that 80% are in favour of this movement.

The Bill, which is just 14 pages long, results from the fact that the Supreme Court ruled over a year ago that criminal law prohibiting assistance in dying in fact limits the right to "life, liberty and security of the person" as guaranteed under Section 7 of the Charter of Rights and Freedoms.

The new bill calls for "a permissive regime" by which a "competent adult person who has a grievous and irremediable medical condition that causes enduring suffering that is intolerable to the individual" has a right to medically-assisted dying.

The tension now will be to reconcile those who might be at risk in a permissive regime and those who earnestly seek assistance in dying. It hopes to establish a degree of consistency across and within provinces and territories, and support the underlying values of the Canada Health Act.

At the same time it recognizes robust safeguards against abuse are needed, and respects the personal convictions of health care providers.

Good leaders lead: this is necessary and good, but they also try not to get too far ahead of what their population is thinking. Public discernment of what is right, just and good evolves over time. The Supreme Court of Canada, in which I have a lot of confidence, unanimously struck down the ban on assisted suicide in a "charter" case entitled "Carter vs Canada," in 2015. For myself, I have an "advanced care directive" downloaded from the U of T Centre for BioMedical Ethics, filled out in 2004 and updated in 2014, which outlines what treatments I wish and do not wish in my final illness.

It is merely a guideline for my family and medical personnel and has no force in law. However, doing it does concentrate the mind!

Of the four dearly-loved persons who have died in my close circle, three of those illnesses and deaths have been mercifully brief, relatively without pain and not prolonged, and they occurred within a time frame which allowed us all grief, some preparation, and much tenderness.

The fourth death, that of my greatly admired and cherished father, was of the kind that drives one to think about assisted death. He had Alzheimer's disease for ten long years, and died a shadow of the person he had been. It was the eighties, and the idea of hastening his death never entered our thoughts for an instant. And he couldn't tell us.

That is my experience. I seek to listen to that of others. One just has to raise this issue in a small group to hear harrowing stories of prolonged suffering, as well as impassioned pleas against "euthanasia."

We no longer are a death-denying culture, and that, all would agree, is devoutly to be wished.

Death and Dying in Canada: Bill C14 May 12, 2016

Now, in 2016, an emerging set of values and circumstances has brought to our society the poignant and unavoidable question of passing a law that enables a suffering person to be medically assisted in bringing about his or her own death. The deepest moral convictions of each of us must be found, reflected on and articulated.

C-14 in its present form has its supporters and its critics. Its supporters say it is a first attempt to bring in needed legislation providing a federal framework to permit medical assistance in dying. I notice that both physicians and nurse practitioners are mentioned, as are pharmacists in their role of providing assistance.

Its critics say it doesn't include important provisions which the Supreme Court pointed to. It denies the right to minors, even if mature, and excludes prior advance arrangements even after a dementia diagnosis. It includes the restrictive phrase a "reasonably foreseeable death" which "takes in to account all the medical circumstances without requiring a specific prognosis as to length of time a person has to live." So it is cautious. Seen as an end-of-life option, the Bill promises to review all data in five years' time, and promises further study of the three aspects which are being objected to.

Politically, the Prime Minister has called for a "free vote" in Parliament: he has to court some Conservative MPs if the Bill is to pass.

The advocacy group Dying with Dignity hopes now to lobby Senators to insert amendments. In fact, recently, because of intense suffering and that fact that requirements have been met, four exemptions for assisted dying have been granted by Canadian courts in anticipation of the coming changes.

A physician of my acquaintance tells me he thinks 30% of doctors would participate in assisted death, were it de-criminalized. He also believes a very tiny fraction of sick people would choose to exercise this right. Statistics seem to bear him out. In Oregon, where medically assisted death was legalized in 1998, the number of people seeking it were 16 in 1998, and 60 ten years later.

Nurses trained to heal and to prolong life struggle with the issue, just as society is doing, and there is a diversity of views. The Canadian Nursing Association endorses the bill cautiously. The Registered Nurses' Association of Ontario recently held an intense one-day session, examining all the attendant issues. Feelings ran deep.

There are the concerns of vulnerable populations. The bill recognizes "that there are inherent risks which can be identified and substantially minimized by a carefully-designed system imposing strict limits that are scrupulously monitored and enforced."

Requests for medical assistance in dying must be made in writing, witnessed by two independent persons, and there must be a second medical opinion. The person must know that their request can be withdrawn at any time.

Internationally, there are 8 jurisdictions with legal rules for medical assistance in dying. Four are U.S. states (Oregon, Vermont, Washington and California), and the countries of Colombia, Belgium, the Netherlands and Luxembourg. In the Canadian bill, persons would have to be eligible for health services funded by the government. No medical tourism here.

As I wrestle in conscience with this issue, I must say I look in vain for nuanced guidance from my church. The Cardinal Archbishop of Toronto, Thomas Collins has said, "Assisted suicide leads us down a dark path. It is a grim reality," and "A serious threat to families worldwide."

I can't agree.

A further area in need of urgent attention is the extension of palliative care, which is now available to only 30% of Canadians. The preamble to the bill pledges this.

Minister of Justice Jody Wilson-Raybould needs wisdom, courage and a steady nerve right now.

Let's let her hear from us.

Making a Meaningful Doll
May 19, 2016

The first thing I notice was a large room filled with youth sitting comfortably cross-legged on the carpeted floor. Attentive.

Amanda McInnes, who teaches grade 7/8 at St Catherine School in Peterborough, had experienced distress over the murdered and missing Indigenous women in Canada and wanted to bring her students to a new and impassioned awareness of the dilemma.

But it couldn't be just via "head-talk" in order to have an impact. Or even talks and films. Then Amanda went to a teachers conference and heard about the "Faceless Dolls" project. Intrigued, she applied for a small grant from the Ministry of Education and set about making it come alive here. Encouraged by Sherry Lajoie, who is a student achievement consultant with the PVNCCDS Board, and by St Catherine principal Shelley Adair, Amanda went to work planning an interactive day. She invited classes and groups from other schools to come to the Board Office for a day.

Responding were Jen Riel and her dance class from St. Peter's, Colleen Crawley and her social justice group Saints Action from the same school, occasional teacher Mary Dalli from Holy Cross, and others.

On the wall of the room are large posters, a picture of Pope Francis, a summary of the social justice principles of the Catholic religion, and the Seven Grandfathers Teachings on native wisdom. There is the motto "Achieving Excellence in Catholic Education Through Learning, Leadership and Service."

Liz Stone, an educator from the Niijkiwendidaa Native Womens Centre on Water Street, and the parent of a teenager, spoke movingly about the numbers of missing and murdered aboriginal women, a number that keeps increasing as awareness builds. Said Stone to the group, "There is no such thing as a stupid question. Ask away. Even seeking to know is a kind of resistance."

Anne Taylor, a cultural educator from Curve Lake, told the story of two women she personally knew who have died or disappeared. On hand were three other Indigenous leaders to answer student questions. Then bannock, made by the foods class at Holy Cross Secondary School, with jam and butter for all.

The materials were laid out. The students picked up a paper plate, eyed the materials and chose what they wanted to design and glue their doll. I had never worked with a glue gun before!

There were felt figures in various skin tones, hair, dresses, ribbon, beads, yarn, leather, bits of fur, feathers and Metis sashes. But all were to be faceless. All were meant to honour missing women and in a sense rescue them from anonymity.

The Faceless Dolls project was initiated in 2013 by the Native Women's Association of Canada. It is emotionally involving, original and age-appropriate. The activity drew on the students' current knowledge and expanded on it. It responded to their thirst for justice. Many students made more than one doll. McInnes was helped by a volunteer, a dedicated seamstress Sandi Moledski who had, for six years, a shop and studio in Selwyn.

At the end of the day, the dolls, some 350 in number, no two alike, were mounted on large display boards, ready to be exhibited in school lobbies, and in public places, too.

At Holy Cross next door, there is a Medicine Wheel Garden, planted with native species and herbs. The students gathered there at the end of the day to reflect on their experience. I could hear the dance class mulling over what they could create as a choreographed response.

For the teachers, the students and the Native leaders, it was mission accomplished, after six months of planning. Eighty-two students and a score of community members had benefited. The Faceless Dolls Project could be replicated too.

Walk a Mile
May 26, 2016

It's been years, if ever, since I wore really high heels. I was a tall teenager anyway, and I listened to those physical education teachers who warned us, rightly, about lower back and foot and knee problems emanating from the wearing of high heels.

But there I was, a few days ago, fitting into 3-inch heels in bright-red patent leather, on the floor of The Venue, and wobbling around just like everyone else.

It was the breakfast-cum-fitting event put on by Walk a Mile in Her Shoes, the highly successful benefit walk which draws more and more people every year. Peterborough's Walk, organized by the YWCA to support its Crossroads Shelter, will take place at noon, May 27 in downtown Peterborough.

Started in 2001 in California by marriage and family counsellor Frank Baird, the activity caught on quickly. The first time, a few men tottered around a park. Now, it is all over North America, and even Britain, having been brought to Canada by the Calgary YWCA in 2001 and here in 2009. It has many elements: men's initiative and the recognition that violence against women and girls is not a women's issue, creativity and fun, education, solidarity and symbolism. Since 2009, 2000 walkers, all male, have completed the journey, many young, and many high schoolers.

Lots of hairy legs and wide smiles.

I spoke with a young man carrying a briefcase who told me he was a Royal Bank employee coming for the first time. I saw teams of employees from the Probation and Parole office and from the New Canadians Centre. I saw heavy-set men with fetching white sox, shoving feet into red heels. I spoke with a young man who will walk carrying his four-month-old daughter on his chest. He assures me he will practice and be steady.

This year, marking its 125 anniversary, the YWCA has invited 125 women to participate, hence the rows of shoes being signed out at breakfast. Four hundred walkers are expected to take part.

The cost of the red shoes is being underwritten by Nightingale Nursing Registry, a first-time sponsor. After the walk, the shoes are cleaned up by volunteers and stored in the basement of the Y.

Executive director Lynn Zimmer points out that it starts out in laughter, but soon moves to empathy and understanding. Walking in those dang shoes is uncomfortable. However, there a serious purpose. Half of all women have experienced at least one incident of harassment, some serious sexual assault. About every six days in Canada, a woman is killed by her intimate partner. Any given night, 3300 women and children are in shelters across the country, having fled their homes in fear. And only 22% of incidents are reported and investigated, so the real numbers are higher.

After the walk comes the talk, the YWCA hopes. What are the causes of all this misery? What can the individual do? How safe can we make the future for our girls, our daughters? What do celebrities, their ways, their dress, their songs and their views have to do with situation? How does the socialization of boys and young men have to change?

"It will take both genders working together to make a dent in this," says Zimmer.

The schools, the parents, the churches and religious institutions, the justice system and the arts all have a heavy responsibility. We have inherited a long history; let's say 5000 years, of women's second-class status, of men's superiority and right to dominate.

Lynn herself, is wearing ankle-high, bright-red canvas running shoes. "This is my footwear!" she laughs. And for me, the plan is half a mile in heels, half a mile in red flats.

All the while keeping in mind Raptor Jonas Valanciunas and his bad ankle.

Daniel Berrigan: Presente!
June 2, 2016

Gather round, all you readers under 50 years of age who are interested in the political/religious history of the United States of America in the 20th century. Who could deny the pre-eminent place that religion continues to play, for both good and ill, in American politics in the 21st?

Daniel Berrigan, S.J. played his heroic part in the sixties and seventies, a time of great upheaval: the civil rights struggle and the Vietnam War, violence abroad, and violence in the streets and on the campuses at home.

He was my friend, I am proud to say, who would come to Montreal frequently, meet a handful of progressive Vatican 11 Catholics, visit Loyola College for poetry readings, and celebrate mass in someone's living room.

Dan died May 1, at age 94 at the Jesuit House in New York. Although notorious as an active protestor of the war in Vietnam and after having been arrested, tried and serving three years in federal penitentiaries, he wanted neither to lead a movement or to be a celebrity. He was enduringly critical of America's cult of personality, consumerism and aggression, right up to the last.

He entered, with his brother Phil and a few others, the draft office in Catonsville MD in May, 1968, presented flowers to the clerks there, took piles of draft records to the parking lot and set them ablaze with homemade napalm. It sent shock waves around America.

Here was a highly-educated Roman Catholic priest, a chaplain at Cornell University in Ithaca, NY and a counsellor to students there, committing acts of civil disobedience. He was counselling young men to refuse to respond to draft notices, the war being unjust and he could no longer stand aside as they did so and courted arrest.

When he refused to give himself up and went on the lam, there was the tragic-comic sight of FBI agents, almost all Irish-American Catholics, taking him in somewhat sheepishly. The war was a proxy one in a Cold War setting. There was no formal declaration of war. South Korea was the client of the U.S. and France. Its capital, Saigon, fell in 1975 to troops from the north, which was sponsored by China. At its bleak end, 1 to 2 million Vietnamese, many civilians, had been killed, along with 58,000 Americans.

Dan's power as a poet moved people immensely. After the Catonsville raid, he said, "My apologies, good friends for the fracture of good order, the burning of paper instead of children, the angering of the orderlies in the front parlour of the charnel house. We could not, so help us God, do otherwise. For we are sick at heart. Our hearts give us no rest for thinking of the land of Burning Children and of that other child, of whom the poet Luke speaks." He went on, "We have chosen to say with the gift of our liberty, if necessary our lives, that the violence stops here, the suppression of truth stops here, this war stops here."

Berrigan lived on, a true prophet. He said not long ago, "Until women are fully integrated into this church, every time I go to the altar, I feel compromised."

But with the Iraq and Afghanistan incursions, he was deeply disheartened about America.

Still, one of the fruits of his efforts can be seen today, May, 2016, a direct link between his ardent, faith-based resistance of the 1960's and 1970's, and a recent statement from the Vatican that the RC church is pulling back from its 1200-year-old "just war" doctrine.

When my spouse died in 2013, I asked Dan what he thought suitable to be written on John's headstone. "Two words," he said: "Amen, Alleluia." It seems to me they could now be written on his.

Celebrate Service
June 9, 2016

This is my "sunny ways" column, inspired by the story of the recent benefit concert in Sydney N.S. for Fort McMurray. Twenty-five hundred people came to the arena to hear musicians such as the *Barra MacNeils* and the *Men of the Deeps*. It raised $250,000. Sydney itself knows all about hard times.

Today, as I drove home from the Honda dealer in my safe car, sagging tires replaced, I reflected on the number of people in this town who cheerfully serve me in many ways. They provide a very high quality of life.

It's not Thanksgiving, but I want to express thanks anyway. And now.

There are Cindy and Mike at Honda, and mechanic Terry, who showed me how to use one of those portable compressor units to blow up a tire in an emergency.

There's Michelle and Bonnie at the Credit Union. They smile and make small talk and compensate for my thin technological capacity. They turn the screen around and show me my account on line. I could use an outdoor machine to get cash, but who wants to?

At the eye doctor's office, that of Dr Fernando, there's a South American woman who regularly tightens my sunglasses, and the doctor reassures me that I have only age-related decline.

There's Conor at Pulse Physiotherapy and Scott at Synergystix, who tune this form, almost four-score in years, and keep it somewhat relaxed, which is greatly needed in Blue Jays season. Plus, if you wish, you can have high-minded conversations about books, politics and child care. One day I told Conor I was having a party and had no cocktail shaker. He brought me his to borrow, one of his wedding gifts.

There's Dr. Gibson and Dee, the nurse practitioner, and Beth and Chris. Recently, I met Dr Gibson at a refugee event and another time, singing with the Peterborough Singers.

Who could forget Hani at Shoppers, one of the world's most kind and alert pharmacists? And Marcia at Sears, whose sparkle makes paying almost painless.

For problem ears, Roy Braun once took me in after hours. I had taken two of his accomplished daughters to Jamaica years ago on awareness trips. Hearing is pretty important.

Roy said I have difficulty with high bird sounds. That amused grandchild, Jack, age 12, who said: "If there are any high bird sounds, grandma, look at me: I will flap my arms."

At the library, Kate knows a lot about books. I have learned how to download books from Overdrive, the Ontario Library Service site, and how to use my iPad, all in free lessons.

At Hospice, one of the warmest places in town, a volunteer arranging flowers spontaneously gave me one. The receptionist offered a cup of tea, and showed me the books and stories for the bereaved of any age.

At Trent Athletic Centre, Tony the custodian, and those desk youth who talk sports so knowledgeably, are welcome, familiar faces. Three times a week, I get to enjoy Neli, the personal trainer who cheers on about 100 seniors. At Scotia MacLeod, where my nest egg is stashed, Doug and Gord do their utmost to help me understand the mysteries of the market. Bull and Bear indeed.

At Spokes and Pedals, Sue and Dave serve and fix, equally skilled and friendly.

Spiritually, Fr Leo Coughlin, age 83, has a weekly lunch at Kelsey's for group discussion. The Friday morning meditation group at St. Andrew's Parlour continues week after week.

These are my concrete specifics, but I know that all over Peterborough, different people and different businesses and agencies are doing the very same. Indeed, I venture a guess that, since Canada has 35 million people, leaving out the babies, 31 million of us are doing good deeds every day.

The Canoe and Us
June 16, 2016

The technical part of the presentation had a few glitches, but nothing could hide the potential glory of the proposed Canadian Canoe Museum, outlined to a Peterborough audience on May 26.

If all goes well and the funds......a whopping $50 million, are found: locally, nationally, privately and through governments, this modern, even visionary structure will be started in 2017, which is, after all, the 150th anniversary of Confederation. Such anniversaries are called sesquicentennials. (I promise that's the last time I will use that word).

To cover 100,000 square feet on Parks Canada land right across the water from the Liftlock, and indeed celebrating by contrast the Liftlock's solidity, this museum will complement the achievement of 19th century architecture with 21st century work. (The liftlock was the project of Richard Birdsall Rogers, who began planning it in 1896.)

The building will comprise 80,000 square feet, half for exhibit space and half for other needs: education hubs and workshops, a large multi-purpose room, a café and archive areas, and administration. Chair Bill Morris of the Canoe Museum Board, described the ten-year plan with the phrase "Onto the National Stage."

Indeed it is. The travel website *Travel Advisor* names the Canoe Museum as second among 47 Peterborough places of interest. It is full of high praises from visitors.

Our collection of 650 canoes, kayaks and dugouts needs a permanent home. They are now in a sixty-year-old former warehouse.

The design, by architects Heneghen Peng of Dublin working with Kearns Mancini of Toronto, calls for a 6 metre-high, two-storey construction which fits the contours of the land, with a roof garden accessible from the road.

This area is to be planted with native species so that "a bird will think it's ground" said one planner.

Our varied seasons have been accounted for with waterproof membranes in the roof to prevent melting snow and ice from seeping in. There are such roofs around the world, even in sub-arctic situations. In Toronto, every new building must now have a green roof.

Of the canoes and dugouts, 139 are on display now, all that the space allows. Some hang from the ceiling.

The information night started with sacred drumming by Janet McCue, and a welcome from Curve Lake Chief Phyllis Williams. Aboriginal leaders have been deeply involved in the project.

The canoe is a man-made artifact, each with its own story. It is well-loved and has become emblematic of our Canadian past. "The canoe links us to our past, to each other and to the future," said Morris.

The impressive chair of the selection committee, Lisa Rochon, whose architectural writing has won awards for the Globe and Mail, spoke of the process: 92 submissions from around the world, narrowed down to five finalists, and the choice of Heneghen Peng.

It was good to see Rochon in animated conversation with visionary John Jennings, a retired Trent professor and nationalist, who in as far back as 1986, crossed Canada drumming up support for such a project.

Rochon spoke of the brightness of the design, its serpentine glass wall and the green space outdoors between the building and the water, which is called the Sunday Afternoon Space. I can hardly wait.

"It can be nowhere else but here," Rochon said. "No ground has been lost," said the landscape architect. "I'm overjoyed with that roof."

The website of the CCM is well worth a visit: animated, and informative. This has been a passion for many Peterburians for a long time.

I jotted down on my feedback sheet that the word "museum" just might not capture the project and its potential. I hope it taps in to our environmental consciousness and even gets a bit political, not partisan, but political. I also hope that it will tap into another growing modern phenomenon, that of meditation and inter-spiritual gatherings.

Then I took out a membership.

Refugees: How Are They Doing Now?
June 23, 2016

The roomy kitchen of Miriam's on Aylmer Street is steamy and hot in late May for some three hours, as 14 energetic women: two Syrians, 11 Canadians and one Egyptian-Canadian translator named Suzanne, tackle the making of five hot Syrian dishes and a salad.

For Tamara and Khaldia, who now have a little halting English, it was their way of saying thank you to their sponsors, a group of neighbours who call themselves "Mosaic." Mosaic has been assisting the new arrivals in every way possible: medical appointments, which can be sensitive given Muslim culture, finding halal food (No Frills and Freshco can supply), teaching the kids to ride bikes, and even reassuring them in the middle of the night that the beeping fire alarm just needs batteries.

Mosaic has guided the refugees on climate and customs, taking the women to a Markham mosque to find lightweight summer clothing, and finding equipment for swimming and even tobogganing.

They have become proficient at a Google App which translates Arabic into English and back. Suzanne is peppered with questions. She is laughing and lively. A Melkite-rite Christian from Cairo, she came to Canada 29 years ago, married and made a life here. A generous one, I'd say.

Tamara and Khaldia have arrived in beautiful, black embroidered abayas, which are floor-length gowns, a kind of loose-fitting robe commonly worn in the east. Two small children play and make posters in another room.

Every knife and pot of Miriam's is in action. I look at the huge pile of vegetables: cauliflower, green beans, cucumbers, tomatoes, eggplant, garlic, potatoes, yogurt, green pepper. Things start to steam and bubble, are pressed together, flipped over, seasoned with kosher salt. Some dishes are further baked. The Canadians have a lot of wine, the Syrians not so much, water will do.

The spices come out and are measured by the handful: coriander, salt, turmeric, cardamom and lemon salt (citric acid).

There is an unusual but important spinach-like vegetable which Mary, a Mosaic member, has managed to find at a Pakistani shop called Deccan Bazar on Lansdowne Street. It is called mulakhiyah. From the leaves of the Nalta jute tree, it is dark green, rather like cooked okra. How our mono-cultural city is changing, led of course, by cuisine. There are no written recipes: just look and taste and experiment.

There is also a cut finger, but with two nurses in the crowd, all is well.

Serious chopping continues. Chicken is washed, the rice steamed, all four burners are on the go.

The gender question is perhaps the biggest adjustment challenge for Middle Easterners in Canada. But today, among women, the newcomers relax, laugh, and late in the afternoon, dance.

The Mosaic people decline to refer to their Syrian friends as "my family" or "our family," which would be somewhat paternalistic. There is equality and good humour. One of the Syrian women has suffered the death of an infant before arriving here. Through sign language and a few phrases, and Suzanne's help, a Canadian woman offers some comfort. Universal experiences bridge a divide.

Down at the New Canadian Centre, Michael, co-coordinator of settlement, tells me that about 20 families have arrived here. He works with Tamara Hoogerdyk and three more staff who speak Arabic. Some 15 more families are expected.

Michael is grateful that Peterborough had the lead time it did, unlike major Canadian cities which faced an early and large influx. The NCC could recruit and train volunteers. He has found the work "a vocation" with many good moments: a new baby arriving for the family sponsored by the Rotary Club, and other congenial cross-cultural moments.

"In 20 years, we will look back at this moment in our city with pride," he says.

Towards One School System
June 30, 2016

School's out.

Time to take a deep breath and tackle an issue that has been for a long time simmering here in the Peterborough area: one school system. I'm persuaded it is the right direction in which to go.

I have taught, happily over the years, in public, Catholic and independent schools in our region. All have many virtues. Good teachers and good kids are everywhere. People with vision, caring and brains.

So my proposal is not a critique of any one of them.

92

Let's leave aside the independent schools. They are well-resourced and well-funded by private donors and high fees. They are costly, out of reach of the vast majority of parents. When I returned to Canada after six years overseas, I was keen to teach *Third World Studies*. The headmaster of an independent school saw the benefits of such a course and hired me in 1981. This is the advantage of the independents: flexibility in curriculum and small classes.

But our commitment needs to be primarily to the public schools. The time has come for us in Ontario to adopt one, publicly-funded school system.

A major reason is financial. We are province in great debt: the only one left in Canada which funds four systems: (English Public, English Catholic, French Public and French Catholic). In recent years Newfoundland and Labrador, Manitoba and Quebec have all applied to the Government of Canada for an exemption from the requirement to fund two school systems. It has been quickly granted. We alone are left looking backwards.

One hundred and fifty years ago in the agreement that formed Canada, there were two dominant religious groups: Catholic and Protestant. Funding for two school systems was written in. But Canada in 2016 is not the Canada of 1867.

It is proudly diverse and publicly secular. I like it that way. And I am religious.

Were we to adapt, we would have one School Board and one office, one administration, with as many leaders as it takes, one bus system, and one common curriculum with space for the teaching of all religions. There would be substantial savings.

Charles Pascal, who was president of Fleming College, said, "Providing Catholic education with public money is an anachronism waiting to be brought to an end by a courageous Queen's Park legislature." The United Nations itself has criticized Ontario for funding one religion only, saying it is discriminatory.

We need to take on this political hot potato with composure. Some 60% of Ontarians support such a move. A few numbers: Kawartha Pine Ridge Board has a budget of $386 million, 74 elementary and 4 secondary schools, and 32,000 students. Peterborough Catholic Board has a budget of $174 million, 37 schools and 14,000 students.

Some public schools in our county are closing: some Catholic schools are over-crowded. The systems compete for students.

A more important reason for amalgamating systems is the social unity one. How do we explain to kids as they pass the neighbourhood school why adults cling to an outdated structure?

Each system brings strengths to the table. And weaknesses. Catholic schools, perhaps unconsciously, hold to the idea that they are morally just a bit superior. Under whose direction are they operating: the state or the church? Why the difficulties around sexual questions?

The public schools have given up too much ground on the matter of spirituality, just at a time when we realize how crucial it is to full human development. Many parents are opting for stronger formation in ethics, spirituality and religious knowledge.

Together, all would be stronger. Let's open up the discussion fearlessly and let everyone speak. For the future. For the kids' sake.

Aga Kahn Museum
July 14, 2016

My good friend Cathy works for the federal department of National Heritage and has a wide, deep cultural knowledge, so when she suggests a meaningful outing, I'm in for it.

Couldn't have been more timely, our day recently at the Aga Khan Museum just off the Don Valley Parkway.

A serene, tasteful and subtle complex, open only a few months now, it celebrates all things Muslim, built on a choice site in Toronto.

On 17 acres, on a North York hillside with a view of the CN Tower, it is two structures: one the Museum itself, and the other the Ismaili Centre for Learning. Between the two, elegant, understated buildings are five huge black reflecting pools of water in a welcoming treed park.

It begs the visitor to sit and meditate.

Many cities around the world bid for this centre, which cost $300 million. Toronto was chosen. And for us in Peterborough, it's an easy trip. In fact, our Abraham Festival organizers plan to visit soon.

Funded entirely by the Aga Khan Foundation, it was 12 years in the planning and four years in the building. No expense was spared to create a thing of beauty. The main architect was Japanese, materials came from Namibia and Lebanon, and the director's name is Henry Kim.

Its purpose is to show Islamic art, culture and history, all in a mission to increase cross-cultural understanding and dialogue. What could be more needed in the West today?

Those of us from traditionally Christian cultures readily accept divisions, distinctions and difference within the great religions. In Islam, similar differences exist.

The Ismaili group is Shia, and it has about 15 million adherents. Its inherited 49th Imam, or spiritual leader, is His Highness the Aga Khan who lives in Switzerland. He is fabulously wealthy and a great philanthropist, whose foundation supports education, health and micro-enterprise projects, mostly in Africa and Asia. At Jamaican Self-Help, we were always very impressed with the work and generosity of this foundation.

Light suffuses the museum. There is an interior courtyard and a cantilevered roof which self-shades. Patterned glass screens divide the exhibit areas. At present there are 1000 artifacts, some Qu'rans from 600 years ago.

Islam does not employ and in fact forbids, icons of the divine, so the museum makes use of subtle design, pure materials and simplicity.

In a gracious dining room called Diwan, the menu has been organized by famous chef Mark McEwan, and features Middle Eastern food.

What drew us especially was a talk by Globe and Mail journalist Doug Saunders on his important book *The Myth of the Muslim Tide*. It really should be read by all Canadians.

Saunders mused: "Only in Canada, on a hot summer afternoon, would 350 people gather for a guy named Saunders, introduced by a woman named Stein, to give a talk in a Muslim Centre!"

Careful research has provided Saunders with data showing a troubling gap between what people in different Western countries think is happening with Muslim immigration, and what the facts are. Public perception is wildly wrong. For example, there are 1.2 million Muslims in Canada, out of a population of 36 million people.

In France, the Netherlands and Spain the proportion is 7%. In the UK. 6%. But here are the percentages that people in those countries think the Muslim proportion is: in Britain, 21%, in France 31%, in Italy 20% and in Belgium, 29%.

In the hands of Donald Trump and the Brexit "Leave" politicians, and with so much misperception in the public, "Muslim" has become a term of fear. Facts, not fallacies, are what must guide public policy now, and the attitudes of Canadians.

A treat for us was meeting Saunders, now one of Canada's leading public thinkers, on the very day his insightful column *The Public Meaning of Dallas* was published.

The UN Might Elect a Woman Leader
July 21, 2016

I've been to the United Nations twice in my life.

In the early fifties, my father, seeking, as so many fathers are doing today, to introduce his kids to a wider world than the one we knew, and to encourage us to see it as hospitable, drove us four rambunctious teens from Kirkland Lake (that's north of North Bay) to New York City. By car.

I recall being awed and impressed by our tour of the UN, the size of the General Assembly Hall, and the multi-cultural nature of everyone and everything. Maybe it really did stick, I realize, as I prepare for Peterborough's "Black Lives Matter" rally Friday.

My second visit to the UN, by air, took place in 2000. This time I was sponsored by a Canadian feminist organization to attend meetings which were reviewing the progress for women that had taken place since the huge Beijing Conference on Women in China in 1995. I had been to Beijing, a trip I treated myself to on retiring from high school teaching.

In the process which we were observing, various countries, (called in UN parlance, "States Parties") had to report to the UN about the measures they had taken to enhance women's safety and participation. We from grassroots groups could and did, take issue with official reports. We couldn't speak or shout out, but we had access to our official Canadian representatives, and we corrected them! That was the time of our National Action Committee on the Status of Women led by the eminent Sunera Thobani.

Now again in 2016, I am taking a renewed interest in the UN, because there are 12 candidates running to succeed Ban Ki-Moon as Secretary General, and six of them are women! Historic.

Not only that, but it is a fairly transparent process.

Candidates are presently giving media interviews, answering hard, detailed questions from all parts of the world, and speaking in the General Assembly to promote their candidacy.

If you'd like some welcome relief from the Republican convention in Cleveland, tune in to the UN on Youtube or streaming and meet 12 really impressive people. Surely, meet the women. There is Helen Clark, New Zealand, a front-runner and a plain-spoken leader; Dr Vesna Pusic from Croatia, who has an edge because, if "rotating" the job is important, it is Eastern Europe's "turn" to have an SG. Meet Christiana Figueres, from Costa Rica, a brilliantly fluent woman who, you remember, got the world to agree in Paris last November to a Climate Action Plan. Then meet Natalia Gherman, Foreign Minister of Moldova, and Irina Bokova of Bulgaria, head of UNESCO. And Susana Malcorra of Argentina, her country's Foreign Minister, who is said to have US backing in the contest.

If this is the quality of politician assigned by their country to the UN, I am heartened.

The United Nations is, of course, a huge, costly, bureaucratic and easily-criticized entity. It has 193 member countries, and all have an equal vote, large and small, poor and rich. There is no doubt the big ones attempt to make deals and bribe the poor countries to vote their way.

The Security Council, with responsibility for peace and security, has 15 members, and five are permanent. (The UK, the USA France, China and Russia.) You know which ones, from a western perspective, are endlessly obstructive.

But it is all we have. It has a noble purpose, expressed in the Charter from 1945, when it was signed in San Francisco. At that time, the United States donated land and buildings in New York for its Secretariat. The UN has power and prestige, and has on many occasions accomplished great things; in peace keeping, humanitarian aid, and relationship-building.

All ready for a woman at the helm.
See *www.womansg.org*

Woe in the United States
July 29, 2016

We Canadians who follow public affairs, and that's almost every one of us, are being inundated by coverage of two crucial American political conventions: the Republican one in Cleveland and the Democratic one in Philadelphia. The first was a dangerous farce, without substance or ideas, brought to a new low when Governor Christie of New Jersey led the crowd in a chant of "lock her up!" Echoes of mob mentality: Jerusalem and Berlin come to mind. Who can these delegates be?

With unrelenting bad news coming from our American neighbour related to their festering race and gun issues, we cannot take much comfort. Or feelings of superiority. So many lives lost in so many places. We are frankly appalled at the easy access to guns, access guaranteed by their now-deadly Second Amendment written in 1791. That's 225 years ago. America was a frontier colony, largely rural. Now it is hlghly urbanized and riven by disparity.

When an angry, probably unhinged man has a gun and a grievance, mayhem can follow quickly. When a returned veteran from an ugly experience in Iraq or Afghanistan, who has training in deadly tactics loses his reason, we have mass killings.

With inadequate police training, there are incidents of extreme over-reaction and the use of deadly force as a first response. I was chilled to hear one American police chief suggest that all driver education courses for black youth now should include lessons in what to do when pulled over: put your hands in plain sight on the wheel and be submissive.

The question for our mental health here is how much should we absorb and how frequently. Even more importantly, to whom shall we listen?

Fox News is toxic and bad for your health.

It is owned by the tycoon Rupert Murdoch and his two sons, James and Lachlan. It is bellicose and hard-right. It coarsens public discussion. The viewer gets a ranting Bill O'Reilly or others who make you uneasy about their state of mind. On radio, Rush Limbaugh and Glenn Beck poison public discourse, incite anger, and widen divisions with half-truths which buttress far-right paranoia.

Last year I was with two American women from the deep South who vexed me with their constant denigration of immigrants and their praise of guns in every pocket. Finally I exploded. "Do you only watch that dreadful *Fox News?*" I asked. "Perhaps try *Al Jazeera* for information and balance about the world." As I expected, they blanched. I had turned terrorist before their very eyes. They gave me a wide berth from then on.

CNN is slightly better but their effort to be "balanced" gives legitimacy to the most ridiculous claims of political spokespeople, mostly the Republicans. The USA has no publicly funded broadcaster. PBS is good, but a very small player.

We are relatively well served by the CBC, CTV and Global. I'm not sure if our journalistic standards are by nature better, but we can be thankful for broadcasters with an expressed interest in sound reporting, in outlets which do not seem to have been bought off by advertisers with an agenda. Paul Hunter of the CBC recently expressed his total puzzlement at what is going on in the US. He arrived there two days before President Obama's inauguration eight years ago, to witness the happy conviction that the race question had been settled in America.

Our gun laws are stronger but we need constant vigilance. In race relations, black Nova Scotian writer George Eliot Clarke said at the Lakefield Literary Festival that our country was fortunate in that we had Metis as original people, so "mixed race" was not an insult.

We need to be informed, but also to guard against immersion in soul-destroying comment. Some of my friends "fast" from instant communication and response. Others confine their information-gathering to newspapers.

Wise decision-making and psychological self-defence are called for now.

Foodies on Foot
August 4, 2016

I was never a much of a cook, or interested in food preparation. My mother, bless her, was both. She tried recipes of all kinds, and even subscribed to a book-of-the-month series which sent her a new cookbook every month!

To me she would say, "Rosemary, you just go off to your student council meeting." And so, important skills and knowledge have had to skip a generation. I'm glad to report they have. I see gourmet sons and grandchildren, male and female.

But to help me along, our small city is fast becoming a food hub, filled with interesting and delicious small restaurants, expert chefs and knowing patrons.

Catching the wave is an enterprising young man named Donald Fraser. For five years, because he is both a foodie and an environmental activist, he has organized, largely through his website, popular walking tours, three hours in length, on Wednesday afternoons in spring and summer.

Fraser has two purposes: introduce Peterborians to their own quality resources for dining out, while enabling them to meet other Peterborians whom they don't yet know, and introduce tourists to our culinary treasures.

He has found that the bulk of his customers are indeed from the city, who aren't very familiar with downtown. Now that's astonishing.

Fraser selects restaurants all within the city centre, which make use of local and regional produce.

Spread largely through word of mouth (pun intended), Fraser's culinary walks have attracted many groups of fourteen or fifteen friendly walkers. On the day I went along, one woman was a travel agent treating her best friend to a birthday gift. There was a nurse and her husband from Ennismore, and another woman, a restaurateur herself, about to be married in two weeks time. That gave Lisa Dixon at Black Honey Bakery a chance to present two fresh-made wedding cookies.

Each week, six destinations are featured and there is a talk by the owner or chef, along with meaningful samples of the cuisine featured there.

The six places differ from week to week. Ours involved stops at The Publican House, Two Cooks, The Rare Grill House, Sam's Sandwich Shop and The Night Kitchen, along with Black Honey.

We walked the distance. When I first registered at Fraser's website (*www.ptbolocalfoods.ca*) I saw the title "Farm to Table," and I thought we'd be driving to a farm to start. Rubber boots? But no, it's a pedestrian stroll which includes discovery and delight. At $35 a ticket, I thought at first it is a bit pricey, but the treats, including a jar of homemade pickled beets from Two Cooks, the delicious thin crust pizza from The Night Kitchen and the award-winning craft beer at The Publican House, more than made it a bargain. The new knowledge was worth a lot more. These folks are dedicated to taste buds and to healthy ingredients.

At the Rare Grill House, pride is taken that every part of the cow is used, even the Achilles tendon. For our repast, we had beef cheek, very much as tender as tenderloin. At Two Cooks, Susan told us about a film shoot they had just done for the Food Network: two days of work for seven minutes of finished material.

The Publican House has recently won awards at a brewing competition, and their brews are now sold at Sobeys. Sam's was featuring their Dagwood sandwich during a busy lunch-hour trade.

The restaurant owners in Peterborough are not in great rivalry with each other, Fraser says. They help each other out and cheer each other on.

I'll never be a food critic, nor even a dinner-party thrower of repute, but this summer activity needs to be known about and enjoyed.

Clinton May Clinch
August 18, 2016

We are going through an interminable American presidential election campaign, the most disturbing one in my memory, with its ugliness from the GOP side.

We must still, even in the dog days of summer, pay some attention to the current drama, since our destiny is so closely tied to the American one, for good or ill.

The dates to watch for are Voting Day, Tuesday, November 8, and three television debates, scheduled for September 26, October 9 and October 9. Though long planned by a non-partisan debates committee and agreed to by the parties, Mr. Trump is now making noises that he won't play ball if he doesn't like the moderator (bring on NPR' s Gwen Ifill, please), and he may change the dates if they conflict with NFL football. This man is supposed to be a serious leader.

I am unabashedly pro-Hillary Clinton. I met her friendly self and said hello briefly at the Fourth United Nations Conference in Beijing, China in 1995, when she came as "First Lady" (the American media calls this person FLOTUS (First Lady of the United States) and gave a ringing feminist speech declaring that women's rights are human rights, and human rights are women's rights.

At that historic meeting, there were the official delegations from 190 countries and 35,000 of the rest of us, citizens who had paid our way, told the Chinese government to find us a site, and held our governments to account. Clinton came to our site and buoyed us up.

She is very smart, conscientious and well educated. She has worked for progressive causes (not all of them, but many) for 30 years in public life. She has endured personal humiliation with dignity. Such a choice absolutely must not become fodder for political attack from either left or right.

She is a skilled negotiator, respected around the world. Mr. T has taken a smear campaign to a new low, unleashing hatred we thought impossible in the American psyche.

I ask myself why. Is it pure misogyny? Dislike of her spouse? Her wealth and the high fees she charges to give speeches? Jealousy?

One can call her a villain and avoid looking at her policy platform. That's diversion writ large. The charges made so virulently against her honesty and competence have been repeated and outrageous.

But wait: there is a Pulitzer-prize-winning site called *Politifact*, a project of the newspaper The Tampa Bay Times. (*www.politifact.org*). *Politifact* is exactly the kind of investigative journalism one hopes for. Do the research impeccably and then publish the results. Respect the voter's intelligence.

And it is a fun site. It traces the assertions made by candidates, and it calls Clinton the most honest of them all, at 70% truthful. Trump is at 28% truthful.

The Politifact categories are "true," "mostly true," "mostly false," "false" and "pants on fire." One can do the categorizing oneself of Mr. Trump's recent statement, "Obama founded ISIS."

The charges about Clinton's honesty have been thoroughly put to rest by conservative commentator Jill Abrahamson, who was editor of the *New York Times* and writes for the *Wall Street Journal.* In May, she wrote, "I have launched investigations into Clinton's business dealings, her fundraising, her foundation and her marriage. She is fundamentally honest and trustworthy."

And Abrahamson continues: "There are no instances I know of where Clinton was doing the bidding of a donor or benefactor."

Clinton has policies: on the Supreme Court, on climate change, on health care, on trade, on terrorism, on guns and on taxes, to mention some. We can hope these become the focus of attention in the next three months.

My American friends have taken to wearing these T-shirts: "I am not crazy about Hillary...but I am not CRAZY!"

A Winter Spent Preparing for a Journey to Russia September 15, 2016

How did it come to this? At my age, that I should start out to visit that place which Winston Churchill, in some frustration in 1939, called "a riddle wrapped in a mystery inside an enigma."

I am just plain curious that's all. It has nothing to do with Vladimir Putin, except that I hope he doesn't invade Latvia this year. Or any year.

It has to do with learning something about the long turbulent history of the world's largest country, about heroic human bravery and suffering, and about renowned artistic achievement. It has to do with my endless questions about the reasons for Russian attachment to authority and dictatorial men, and at the same time Russians' enduring loyalty to the Orthodox Christian faith among its ordinary people.

This huge land running through both Europe and Asia, thousands of kilometers in breadth, with 150 million people, bisected by the Arctic Circle, has a very cold northern climate and a sub-tropical one too (i.e. the Olympics at Sochi, 2014).

I want to explore Russia's poetry and novels and plays, its glorious music and dance, and its achievements in science and architecture. I long to see the Moscow subway, all stations said to be works of art, and those onion-domed churches. There are actually four Orthodox cathedrals inside the Moscow Kremlin walls.

But what about its treatment of dissenters, its gulags and its suppression of alternative opinion? Could I meet a hero of mine, Edward Snowden? And Russia's recent sports scandals. Its support of Bashar al Assad? How does one square it all?

Choosing Russia as a destination has given me a winter of concentrated learning: I've devoted several months to reading and films and youtubes and music listening. I've met Russian students at Trent, and Olga at the New Canadians Centre. I've emerged eleven books later, the best of which was *Natasha's Dance*, Russia's cultural history. And the irreplaceable fiction. I think one learns best through fiction. I really felt the awfulness of the siege of Leningrad (1941-42) by the Germans: one million dead of starvation.

Nine movies later, from the silent films of Sergei Eisenstein to the searing look at rural poverty in *Leviathan* (2014), I have a smattering of knowledge, not systematic or scholarly, but sincere and deeply-felt, of Russian reality. Still keen to go.

With my bridesmaid from 55 years ago, I've planned the travel. Being past the stage of backpacks and hostels, we found a river cruise with a Nordic company that was the first to start tourism into Russia in 1997. They assured us that they monitor the political and military situation closely. Mr Putin, after all, has been making aggressive gestures towards countries on his western borders.

The first hurdle has been overcome, the visa, but that took 3 bus trips to Toronto. Russia has outsourced this visa process from its Consulate to a private firm on St. Clair Avenue. There, a worker behind glass examined my printed application form, a copy of which I had already emailed. It asked for my education and employment, going way back.

Then there is the $150 fee in cash, and the passport photo, but not the size that the CAA provides: much smaller. I am referred to a basement photographer down the street. He laughs and tells me he knows exactly what Russia requires. He also says, "You wouldn't believe how many people planning to go to the Sochi Olympics gave up because of the complications of this process."

I persist. The clerk at the window says she will correct my application form for $30 more in cash. I pay. My friend in the US has paid $350 dollars to hire some outfit to do her Visa work.

Maybe she's the smart one. But we're going. Just don't announce I'm a journalist.

Discovering the Changes in Russia First Hand September 22, 2016

In my quest to understand just a bit of the Russian reality before departure in August, I spend some time acquiring a few Russian words.

"Thank you" is "spasiba," and "please" is "pozhalusta" and "mother" is "mama," and "home" is "dom." "Nyet" is of course, "no." I'm almost good to go.

There is the helpful website Duolingo. Apparently teachers are making use of Duolingo, and a friend Nansi said her 8-year-old picked up some Spanish via this program. It knows that all kids like to learn via the computer. Me too.

There is a list of words and expressions painstakingly printed out for me by Daria and Anna last winter, Russian students at Trent.

The Cyrillic alphabet does not yield up any ready meaning for me. Russia and many other countries use the alphabet, which was designed in 900 by a Christian Orthodox missionary to what is now the Czech Republic. A monk named St Cyril.

It has 32 letters and many are based on Greek capital letters. I can recognize the P, C, T, X, K and M, but that doesn't help in the reading. Still, 250 million people use the Cyrillic alphabet. My name Rosemary looks like this PO3M, (reversed e), P, (reversed N).

While travelling, I underwent two more language lessons, but everyone else in the class was quicker. So I said "dobre utra" everywhere I went, whether or not it was indeed morning.

The recent history of Russia fascinates anyone, and the travellers who most enjoyed this trip were the historians among us.

The Soviet Union dissolved on Christmas Day 1991, when the leaders of three member republics, the Ukraine, Belarus and Russia herself told President Mikail Gorbachev, who had readied the ground for such movement himself by promoting openness and restructuring, that they were leaving. He resigned and handed over leadership to Boris Yeltsin.

Do you know that 13 other associated republics followed suit? It was humiliating for the central government, and may account for Mr Putin's modern threats to re-acquire some of these territories. The new entity was renamed "The Russian Federation" and got a new flag, which is white, blue and red, with no hammer and sickle or red star.

While we in the West rejoiced at this turn of events, Russia then suffered a great economic collapse, which has only recently been somewhat reversed.

A poll taken in 2014 showed that 57% of Russians, mostly older folks, regret the break-up, while 30%, mostly younger, are enthusiastic about new freedoms and opportunities. To switch from state control to capitalism and the market economy without regulatory systems or enough human capacity has been a great difficulty, enabling a few Russian hustlers to become vastly wealthy, and most others to stagnate. The annual per capita income in Russia is $10,000 USD. (Canada's is $43,000).

I'm told there is more freedom of expression. "We get BBC and CNN. Criticism is now possible," one Russian told me. "There are political magazines and papers of all kinds." But Amnesty International expresses real concern about growing repression. I read with horror of the unsolved assassinations of liberal reformer Boris Nemtsov (2014) and journalist Anna Politkovskaya in 2006.

It is complicated, for sure. Yeltsin was called by the BBC "the flawed founder of Russian democracy." Elections are said to be free and fair. Vladimir Putin, who came from the KGB and the mayorship of St Petersburg, heads the United Russia Party. There are other parties, one being the Communist Party. The parliament, called the Duma, has 448 members. Putin, elected in 2000, was re-elected for a six-year term in 2012.

I sometimes think my head is splitting from the contradictions. As I admire and enjoy being here, I sense some of the old convictions of my Cold War mentality sliding away. With major "buts."

Those Odious Ads
September 29, 2016

I interrupt my series of stories on Russia to tackle once again the objectionable activities of a Calgary group, one I'd describe as anti-choice fanatical, who call themselves the "Canadian Centre for Bio Ethical Reform."

Beware of Orwellian titles that sound scholarly or benign.

The group is going, small city by small city, across Canada with its in-your-face, anti-choice activism. Peterborough is now on its radar. We are to be confronted with ugly and demeaning ads purchased and placed on the backs of our buses and other public places soon.

We in Peterborough have earned both positive and negative cross-Canada fame in recent years. Think fire at the mosque and our response, then the small plane landing on Lansdowne Street, and the cats-on-leashes bylaw.

This time we may be infamous for having bent to the threatening tactics of CCBR.

If we thought that abortion is a settled matter in Canada where social peace has been achieved, we are wrong. Although decriminalized by the Supreme Court in 1988, and a right supported by a vast majority of Canadians, the issue continues to simmer among far-right politicians and religious leaders.

It is still highly politicized in our country. Joyce Arthur of the highly-regarded Vancouver-based Abortion Rights Coalition of Canada which monitors access to abortion, says, "We still have miles to go, and the end is not in sight."

Three months ago, Arthur provided our mayor and Council with constitutional grounds on which to ban the materials of CCBR from public display. But Council chose to cite a poor understanding of "freedom of speech" to undergird its decision to allow the ads.

First of all, the ads contravene the Canadian Code of Advertising Standards. They show three panels, two of which have images of fetuses of indeterminate term, and the third panel covered with a huge splotch of blood. The slogan says "Growing, growing, gone" along with the claim "Abortion kills children. End the killing."

Such a claim is demonstrably false. Under the law, fetuses are not children and abortion is not murder.

110

These ads are not "controversial," they are anti-woman and gender discriminatory. They shame and embarrass pregnant women, and verge on hate speech because of the implication that women are murderers.

It takes some sophistication in both biology and women's studies, and some experience in legal affairs to stand up to such strategies. One can get bullied. One can be frightened by a threat of a suit. Unfortunately, Peterborough Council has approved the sale of ad space on buses to this anti-choice group. We commuters and citizens will be subject to a long period of this material. Yet, buses are publicly controlled and funded. Peterborough has given a third party permission to condemn and mischaracterize abortion, and shame and harass women in their own city.

Let's hope Grande Prairie and Hinton, Alberta, two other cities being bullied by the CCBR, will show more fortitude.

Of course, speech cannot be prohibited on the basis that it is controversial or divisive. But advertising is subject to greater restrictions. It must be accurate and not discriminatory or demeaning. There are other rights protected in the Charter of Rights and Freedoms: protection against discrimination is one. Only women seek abortions. Moreover, the right to speech is not unlimited. In a 2008 decision, a BC court ruled that a woman's right to privacy overrules anti-abortion protestors outside clinics.

Our city could safely have, on all these grounds, refused to co-operate with CCBR. It buckled. Public shaming is not what we do, as a rule. But the fury of "pro-lifers" shows no consideration for a distressed pregnant woman or a troubled teen.

It's time for me to stand up for people of my gender, though considerably younger than I, who have now, or ever, needed an abortion. It's a matter of personal conscience.

111

The Faith of Russian Orthodoxy
October 6, 2016

When I enter a new culture, I'm looking for the underlying values, especially the ones that come from the religious faith of the ordinary people. So here is Part 1 of two parts exploring Christian Orthodoxy, as I observed it in the Russian Federation. And in Toronto.

The long, dramatic story of a religion which has dominated political and spiritual life through ten centuries in Russia is endlessly fascinating. Its outward signs are everywhere: 50,000 churches existed before the October Bolshevik Revolution of 1917, now perhaps there are 10,000. Some are places of worship again, many are restored as museums.

Russians take great pride in these installations which dominate the skyline. They are glowing architectural splendours, with up to 15 onion or helmet-shaped domes, all glistening and gold, or painted in brilliant hues. They stand all over the landscape, rural and urban.

Are they signs of deep faith, sources of national pride, treasuries of ancient artifacts, or monuments to military victory?

Perhaps all of the above.

If we were to look at Canadian religious practice, belief and influence, we would, I think be similarly mystified. We'd draw few conclusions, sociologist Reginald Bibby aside.

The 85-year (1917-1991) story of suppression, nay persecution, of orthodoxy by Lenin, Stalin and Brehznev especially, followed by the modern resurgence since the nineties, is spellbinding.

To go way back, and to witness how embedded Orthodox Christianity is in Russia, recall that in 988, Grand Prince Vladimir in Kiev (now the capital of Ukraine), who ruled a territory then called Rus, sent emissaries to neighbouring countries to bring back reports of other faiths: the Jewish one, the Muslim one and the Christian one. He decided that the dietary laws of Judaism and Islam were too restrictive so the story goes, so he adopted Christianity, had himself baptized and then converted, by order, all his subjects.

Not long afterwards, in 1054, the great schism, a complete break, came between two huge Christian wings: Orthodox in the east, centred in Constantinople (now Istanbul), and Rome, the Roman Catholics, in the west. The schism came about because of differences in geography and language, because of leaders' struggle for power and supremacy, and, here and there, because of a bit of theology: namely the burning question of the kind of bread, leavened or unleavened, to be used for the Eucharist.

We have just lived through the first official reconciliation of these two proud wings of Christianity. It is astonishing to realize that, just this year in February 2016, in Havana, Cuba, the Roman Catholic pontiff Francis, and the Russian Orthodox Patriarch Kirill, met for the first time in 1000 years. Some feuds do go on.

The location for their cordial meeting was chosen because both leaders would be in the southern hemisphere, and because the site was far from old conflicts. They embraced each other and issued a statement saying that they had had shared unity during the first millennium after Jesus, and they regretted the differences which had torn them apart.

We in the West pride ourselves in having achieved separation of church and state in our politics. In the East, no such claim of separation of church and state was ever made. But look at the U.S. election right now. One wonders if this pride of ours has any basis.

113

Finding Passion in the Religion of Russia
October 13, 2016

Orthodox Christian church and the various ways in which Russia has been governed were deeply intertwined. The Tzars, from 1400 on, claimed a divine right to rule and were crowned in cathedrals. They built new churches, usually dedicated to the Virgin Mary, when great battles were won, such as that against Napoleon and the French invaders in 1812. Do you know that Napoleon's proud Grande Armee came to Russia for a mere six months, lost 400,000 men and was outwitted by the Russians who left Moscow empty, some of it burning, and practised a scorched earth policy as they withdrew?

Of course the suffering from resulting food shortages affected both sides harshly.

Moving forward 100 years, at the time of the Bolshevik revolution of 1917, there were 50,000 churches in Russia. But the Soviet leadership had officially adopted the conviction of Karl Marx in Germany that "religion is the opiate of the people."

The wholesale burning and bombing of churches and monasteries, and the execution of bishops and priests, left about 7000 churches remaining in the country. Religious practice was banned and despised. You couldn't be a Christian and be a member of the Communist party.

Who then tended the faith? The old women, they say. What is in the heart of people is not so easily erased.

I was keen to attend a service (in English if possible). So in Toronto in August, I went to the Russian Orthodox Cathedral of Christ the Saviour on Manning Avenue in the Annex. I was greeted by a friendly man in a cassock who told me he was the deacon, and he preached the homily. He said he was a convert to Orthodoxy from Anglicanism, and had found great spiritual treasures there.

The nave of the church was filed with religious icons and banks of candles. One could purchase tapers for .50 at the back and light them as one meditated in front of a picture. I entered into this ritual with gusto. I bought several candles and lit them, thinking of my grandchildren. I learned to bless myself right to left. I didn't kiss the icon but I bowed my head.

There was constant movement, as the celebrant, up behind the iconostasis, a screen covered with five rows of religious paintings, went on celebrating the Eucharist. He brought the bread and wine out through a door in the screen. It was suggested to me that I not approach to take communion since I was not of the Orthodox faith.

A lot of young people were there too, the women with scarves on their heads but otherwise in thoroughly modern Canadian clothing. I bought an Orthodox cross, which has three bars across the main stem. The top bar recalls the satiric sign put over Jesus' cross by Pontius Pilate, naming him "King of the Jews." The middle bar is the usual one of the Christian crucifix, and the third bar is slanted, and stands for the two thieves on either side, Dismas the repentant one, and Gestas, the unrepentant one. In fact, in Kingston, Ontario, from 1894 to 2013, there was a Catholic church called "The Church of the Good Thief," built largely by prison labour.

Russia really represents a biblical encyclopedia. Its thousands upon thousands of icons portray saints and stories from Christian and Jewish scriptures. I would say the best preparation for immersion in Russia is a re-reading of the Bible.

These days there are seminaries bursting with candidates, and monasteries and schools for icon painters and for choir directors. Music is an important part of liturgies. Those deep bass voices stay with me.

The place of religion in a society is, perhaps everywhere, quite ambiguous. Vladimir Putin, present leader of Russia, is demonstrating a new-found faith.

Twice since May he has made pilgrimages to the very fount of Orthodoxy, Mount Athos in Greece. He has donated large sums for the restoration of this ancient Orthodox monastery. The lower clergy in Orthodoxy marry but the monks and bishops do not.

I'm horrified to learn Mount Athos admits no women whatever, nor even female animals! Now that seems extreme.

But overall, I found faith practised with joy and fervour by many Russians.

The Beauty of the Art in Russia
October 20, 2016

To my relief, I've been diagnosed. It's Stendhal Syndrome, a psychosomatic condition first recognized by French writer Stendhal (only one word in his name) in the 19th century.

It is experienced by persons who are overcome by beauty, especially beauty in art.

The syndrome is treated regularly by attendants at St Petersburg's State Museum of Art (the Hermitage). It is marked by dizziness, palpitations and sometimes hallucinations. All these things I experienced in my two days walking some of the 380 glorious rooms of the Hermitage. But I fought back the symptoms on my own.

A photo taken of me in front of Rembrandt's "Prodigal Son" shows the delight of a baby.

Beauty, Russian writer Fyodor Dostoevsky said, will save us. If so, look to Russia.

One of the world's jewels, the Hermitage receives 2500 visitors a day. I think I stepped on all their toes. There are five linked buildings along the embankment of the Neva River. Each one elicits gasps of pleasure.

In one room, portraits of 300 Russian generals during the war against Napoleon. In others, Italian, Dutch, Spanish and German masters. Two Da Vinci Madonnas.

Empress Catherine the Great (1764) must have stripped Europe of its best works. She purchased 3000 paintings. And how would you like to live in a city with 382 bridges?

The website, *www.hermitagemuseum.org* is splendidly organized, taking you to paintings and explaining them.

Later, I'm in the Moscow subway, crowded and fast, a system with 199 stations buried deep at 33 metres beneath the earth's surface. I've descended precipitous escalators, and sped quickly into a subway car. They arrive every two minutes. Nine million Muscovites use the system every day. It has cost me sixty rubles ($1.20), and I can ride all day.

The people look like people in the Toronto subway, perhaps a little less dressy. Sasha my Russian guide and I, have been talking about poetry. He smiles and says, "This is not a set-up. Let me just ask this woman sitting here to recite some of her favorite poetry." He explains to a patient Russian commuter that he has some visitors who don't believe that everyone on the street can recite poetry. She smiles and offers us these lines from national poet Pushkin.

"But now I know while beauty lives,
So long will live my power to grieve."

She continues with 16 lines from heroine-poet Anna Ahkmatova.

Could a Canadian on the street do the same? I ask my neighbour on Manning Avenue. "Maybe Flanders Fields," she says. "Or some Leonard Cohen. Or some Tragically Hip."

Many subway stations are works of art. Stalin, who started them in the thirties, believed that art should be available to the masses. The Mayakovskaya station, with its graceful columns of pink marble and its 35 niches, was an air raid shelter during the Great Patriotic War.

117

The Ploshchad Revolyutsil station features 76 huge bronze sculptures of farmers, athletes, writers and children. As everyone does, I rub the nose of the bronze dog for good luck.

There is the peaceful park in St Petersburg where women are placing flowers at a corner site. In 1941, Sasha tells me (as if 1941 were yesterday), during the ghastly siege, the composer Shostakovich gathered the surviving members of the Leningrad Symphony to perform his 7th symphony. Only fourteen of 90 musicians were left. Here, they defied the Nazis with music.

Music, mostly deep male basses, can be heard everywhere: there are concerts, both classical and pop, of Russian composers, Tchaikovsky, Stravinsky, Rachmaninoff, and even the feminist punk group Pussy Riot and crooner Peter Nalitch. There is the exquisite Bolshoi Ballet in Moscow, and the whirling of Cossack dancers.

When someone says Russia is more cultured than we are, one should probably agree.

Finland the Fabulous
October 27, 2016

Readers have come with me through four Russian articles over the past month. Thank you, Spasiba.

Now here's an afterword from Finland, which shows my true, down-to-earth colours.

We started out for home from Russia via Helsinki, Finland, taking a speedy three-hour train trip from St Petersburg and going through border formalities on the train, half way.

Finland is a society to be greatly admired: 5 million people, a very high standard of living, a welfare state, and the best educational results in the world. With a high degree of friendliness. Plus, it shrewdly negotiates its foreign affairs by having a non-aggression pact with Russia since 1948, and declining to join NATO, though it is a member of the EU.

But I digress. This is all about meeting a Finnish celebrity.

My family admits I do have an eye for faces. In the hotel lobby, I see a fine-looking young Finn. I say to myself: "Hockey player! Now, which one: Jari Kurri? No, he's retired. Teemu Selanne? No, he's bigger. Aha, I remember now, Saku Koivu!"

Eureka.

The captain of the Habs for ten full years, the first European in this role, Koivu became a well-loved figure in Montreal. He suffered and recovered from cancer, and then returned to a nine-minute standing ovation in the Forum, where we went on to play at a high level. He won the NHL Masterston Trophy for courage and dedication in 2002.

Now I, being past the age of selfies, nonetheless approach him for an autograph. He seems pleased, in his own country, to be recognized by a Canadian fan. His teammates all around are vastly amused. They are preparing for the World Cup of Hockey with an exhibition game against the rival Swedes that night.

My hand is still smarting from his firm handshake, but my sons, all beer-league players here in Canada, are delighted. One says on FB: "My mother goes to great lengths to see one of the world's great civilizations, and comes home with a hockey story."

Oh well, it all goes with a full life.

To Finland, attention should be paid. It has had two women prime ministers and it manages to get along with Russia next door. Before the Russian revolution, Bolshevik leader Vladimir Lenin spent some time in Finland, and when he became supreme leader, as a gesture of thanks, he granted Finland independence. That's only 100 years ago.

As I stroll Helsinki, I see a sign promoting a noon-hour concert, the music of composer Jean Sibelius performed by young musicians.

I wander in, to be greeted by a general manager enthusiastic at a Canadian arriving, and mentioning that the Toronto Symphony had Finn Jukka-Pekka Saraste as conductor for ten years. Saraste had been given the keys to the city. I'm happy about that.

The Finns are environmentally advanced. A new Lutheran church has been dug into a rock, not built skyward. Energy-wise, they are at 24% renewables, and heading to 31% by 2020. They are, as an aside, the world's heaviest coffee drinkers.

And, Canadian teachers, here is a rundown of Finnish principles of education: start at age 7, and have 75 minutes of recess a day. No evaluations at all the first six years, and one mandatory test at age 16. All children in the same class, and science classes limited to 16 students to enable experiments to take place. Teachers are highly regarded and are required to have a master's degree.

Finns have a worldwide reputation for great design (i.e. the Toronto City Hall by Viljo Revell). To prove the point, I buy myself a Marimekko blouse.

All hail to Saku and to Suomi.

Recovering from Trumpism
November 3, 2016

As we limp, relieved but disheartened, towards the end of the chilling American presidential campaign, it may be a good time to assess our differences from that great and wounded culture to our south.

American society has been very influential in shaping us in obvious ways, but it is now markedly different from the nation we have become. This needs sober analysis as we reach our 150th birthday, and they mark 241 years.

Of course we aren't voters, but we were shocked and often paralyzed for weeks by the daily infusion of ugly campaign rhetoric and frightening events. My son in B.C. went on a "trump-fast" so disgusted had he become. I think that is pretty typical of us Canadians.

So few Americans seemed to be standing up to Mr Trump. The media, corporate-controlled as they are, were uncritical from the beginning, hiding behind a mistaken notion of journalistic balance, giving Mr Trump soft landings, but at the same time giving him wall-to-wall coverage. From his opening speech about Mexicans being rapists, a sensible citizenry expected the media to challenge his very candidacy.

The craven Republican leadership, lusting for power above all else, such people as Representatives Ryan and Mc Connell and Christie and Guiliani abandoned conscience, looking to their own political fortunes and thereby betraying the women of America who were being humiliated and demeaned, while children's innocence was corrupted by the lewd public remarks of a coarse man.

Eighty million Americans, and who knows how many Canadians watched three TV "debates" which were full of unsubstantiated charges and insults, threatening and misogynistic body language, and bluster and egoism.

We reacted with disbelief and nervous laughter.

Indeed, laughter became the best defence. Actor Alex Baldwin did an eerily accurate Trump impersonation on *Saturday Night Live*. Brit John Oliver offered literate raging rants. Our own Samantha Bee demolished Mr Trump's noxious nonsense. I myself participated in that tongue-in-cheek Facebook thing called "Click for a Brick," in which we clicked on a virtual brick and one was installed on the border between the USA and us. Symbolic, that.

Vulgarity and hate seemed ascendant in American politics, and Trump supporters remained stubbornly unmoved by evidence of his profound unfitness for leadership.

121

Now, as America tries to recover from the long assault on civil discussion and the unleashing of hate, it will be, one hopes, listening to its most careful ethical thinkers. Robert Reich, once Secretary of Labour and now a scholar at the University of California, lamented the "poisoning of the well" of public talk.

How does one clean out a well? Franciscan monk Ricard Rohr wrote that "hatred holds a group together much more quickly and easily than love and civility."

The question is what will last from Toxic 2016? What kind of crisis will Americans have? Their democracy came perilously close to collapse, and a main candidate came close to preaching sedition.

Canada, what of us? No reason for smugness. I heard a CBC radio phone-in with several men and a few women, unrepentant, saying they still supported Mr Trump.

Gasp.

It will take vigorous engagement by all of us to preserve and strengthen our common good. It will take polite speech, even when one has impassioned ideas, a strong sense of compromise, a conviction that our behaviour witnesses to the next generation, a search for decent political candidates at all levels, and a calling out of misogyny everywhere.

We Canadian women feel sullied through association with this American campaign, discouraged by the assaults. We must steer an alternate course. It has of course, begun in Canada by feminist federal leaders.

It continued in Peterborough with the 25th annual Persons Day Breakfast on October 25.

Vital Signs: A Snapshot of Peterborough
November 10, 2016

On October 6, an important report on the quality of life in Peterborough, called *Vital Signs*, was published.

It's a great compendium of information about our community, put out by the Community Foundation with co-operation and statistics from 36 agencies and entities, including the City, the United Way, Telecare, Reframe Film Festival, Fleming and Trent, Greenup, Public Health and the Social Planning Council.

It's a keeper, this four-page report, printed in *The Examiner*, and enlivened by graphics and a few figures and percentages. Our population, city and county, is 134,000. Our voluntarism is at an astonishing 54% participation, higher than the national average by ten points. I had a feeling we were extra generous with our time. Look at the hockey coaches alone.

In the Food for Kids program in 49 local schools, 17,000 kids enjoyed a good breakfast. Our green consciousness is relatively high and growing. Thank Susan Sauve and Cathy Dueck here. One of three of us participated in a voluntary program for the environment. That's good because the indefatigable Maude Barlow's new book, which she discussed here on November 2, is called *Boiling Point*.

The darker side of Peterborough: our unemployment rate is at 4.8, but that varies by month. And the jobless rate only registers those who have looked for work in the preceding month. Still, many jobs are minimum wage ones, at $11.25 an hour. This study shows that an individual needs an hourly wage of $17.65 to live a decent life. Imagine how many individuals among us don't make that.

Too many of us pay too much in rent, which is considered to be more than 30% of one's income. 120 people spend overnight in shelters every night, both youth and adult.

On the wait list for social housing are 1543 households. The cost of food for a family of four for one month, has risen from $820 in 2013 to $865 in 2015.

Of concern too, is that only 15 percent of adults meet the required daily physical activity number. This must be a frustration to our doctors and nurses. Get the kids outside and off the screens.

We have 109 km of cycling routes. I've put my bike away for the winter, but I see some brave cyclists out there still. The number of farmers in our County is way down since 1991, from 270 to 85. Amazingly, 56% of us have post-secondary education, a touch higher than that for Ontario as a whole.

But 15% of us live in poverty. Seven thousand people are on social assistance. A woman told me that on October 29 at the Square there was the annual Coats for Kids giveaway, and people lined up from 8.30 am. Our median income is $31,000. Are we as old a community as we believed? Well, 27% of us are over 60, but 24% are under 30. That sounds good.

When it comes to mental health, which society is becoming more aware of, 74% of us responded in 2003 that we felt we were in good mental health. This is down to 67% today. What are the causes of this decline? Let's have a Town Hall on that question.

Is it hard times economically? General demoralization? Worry about global warming? A decline in religious faith? The American election?

So, Vital Signs gives us a mixed but predominantly positive report, which I appreciate having. I just re-read it in preparation for a visit to a local food pantry.

American poet Maya Angelou has said when one knows better, one does better. On this basis alone, the *Vital Signs* report is greatly to be admired.

Vinnies and St Vincent's ~ a Good Fit
November 17, 2016

My long-time friend Frank Romo suggested I might like to spend a half-day at the St. Vincent de Paul Food Pantry on Murray Street.

He was right.

It was edifying to see both the style and the substance of the Food Bank. Leaving aside for a minute the regrettable reality that Canada still needs food banks, this one is exemplary.

Personal interest, a kind word and a caring attitude are the key factors in making a true and meaningful exchange, whether of goods or of spirit. For both sides, actually.

Those Beatitudes, from the Christian gospel, that still have such an effect on the conscience of people worldwide. They are echoed in all the religions. Not in an evangelizing way but in a service way.

Four mornings a week, Wednesday through Saturday, this food depot is run by Client Care coordinator Sue Mazziotti-Armitage. She had been running the St Anne's School breakfast program for kids when she heard about the opening at the newly-renovated St Vincent de Paul location. "I am Italian-Canadian," she said, "and my mother taught us to care for one another."

This morning, 88 clients come. The wait room is pleasantly furnished, and the receptionist Rosemary, friendly and welcoming. Most of the clients have registered previously and demonstrated their need. They have an receipt card, and the card indicates how many people they are feeding. This will entitle them to a number of points to exchange for food of their choice. They can access the food pantry once every four weeks.

The most surprising feature to me was that each client went upstairs with a volunteer, to browse a well-stocked, if smallish, supermarket.

It is run by Steve Woolbridge, an affable and energetic food manager who left similar work at Foodland in Lakefield. "I really enjoy the volunteers here," he said. I had coffee with several of them. Men and women, mostly of retirement age, they have been GE workers, school teachers and office workers.

"I was nervous being alone at the food depot in the basement of my church," a woman told me. "Here, there is constant company and good cheer."

I saw fresh fruits and vegetables, dairy and meat. There was a knock on the back door. In came Ozzie, age 84. "I am the milkman. Every Wednesday, I pick up bags of milk from Kawartha Food Share and bring them over. Good thing I always knew how to milk a cow."

A woman in a parka told me she planned to make a pumpkin pie, as she picked up a tin of pumpkin. "You'll want nutmeg and ginger," I said. Alas, spices are in short supply. She smiles. "I'll make do."

The St Vincent pantry is entirely supported by volunteer money. It gets $1500 worth of food monthly from Kawartha Food Share, which collects food from all over Peterborough and distributes it to six food banks in the city. One brilliant link for this pantry is that it has the financial support of Vinnies Feel Good Shopping on Erskine Avenue. Donations also come from churches: Immaculate Conception, St Peter's, St Anne's and St Alphonsus.

"I got the name of the store from Australia," says Sue, "and at first, some folks were disappointed the St Vincent de Paul name was gone." The first St Vincent was a 16th century French priest with a special call to the poor. The Society now exists in 120 countries.

"We have 1800 clients a month," says Sue. "No lineups outside. We want to offer privacy and dignity. We are a registered charity, audited annually, and we can offer tax receipts. And by the way," she says, laughing, "we can always use more volunteers!"

The Peterborough Theatre Guild: 50 years
November 27, 2016

It's difficult to measure just how influential the Peterborough Theatre Guild has been in shaping Peterborough's values and cultural life over the Guild's proud 50-year history. Safe to say, that influence has been profound.

The PTG, which marks its anniversary this year, has offered local audiences 400 plays, a marvellous record. This season, there will be nine plays, including a children's play in December and a musical in April.

Live theatre is that most lovely and immediate of the arts. If story-telling is the way we figure out the universe and our place in it, then theatre, which tells stories in direct ways to mass audiences, is crucial to human growth and individual decision-making.

Tragedies performed in the theatre show us paths we are warned not to follow, and choices not to make. Comedies and romances suggest possible paths, and demonstrate the importance of laughing at our foibles.

The Greeks knew it, as they flocked to huge stone amphitheatres to watch (and no microphones either), tragedies of immense scale which focused on human greed, stupidity and cowardice, and to watch comedies of a very ribald nature. The ordinary people of medieval England, for whom Shakespeare wrote, stood in the pit of the Globe Theatre in London and expressed their opinion of what they were seeing by boos and cheers, and even rotten tomatoes.

Older Peterburians may remember the contributions of famed novelist Robertson Davies and his talented wife Brenda, in creating drama here in the forties and fifties. The history of the PTG is replete with honoured names: Beth McMaster, Mabel Smith, Finn Gallagher, Andy Harris, Bryan Jones, Richard Hayman, Bea Quarrie, Gwen Hope, Gillian Wilson, Gwen Brown, Syd Waldron, and Dick Beck are some.

Now in 2016, the PTG has a website and 1500 members (annual cost around $55). Jerry Allen is president and Steve Russell of TASS is board chair. Tickets will soon be available online. It is a staggering achievement for a non-profit, community- based cultural enterprise, with no one knows how many volunteer hours donated every year.

Its sole purpose: to enrich lives with new thinking, to deepen understanding and compassion, and, oh by the way, to entertain.

When I was in high school, and this was the fifties, I played in a high-school production of a play by Thornton Wilder, *Our Town*. It was about love, life and death in small-town America. It won a Pulitzer Prize. I think I was Mrs Webb, and I remember I had to iron a lot.

That experience, and literature classes then and later in my schooling, gave me a great gift: a love of stories, those written, spoken and acted.

I was moved this month seeing *Eclipsed* at the Theatre Guild. Patricia Young and Jennifer Gruer chose this harrowing play about young Irish girls, pregnant and outcast, sent to laundries run by the Church because they had been disowned by their families. It shows us the history of the times but also prods us to consider who is shunned today in society.

Last spring there was the fabulous production of *The Buddy Holly Story* directed by the gifted Jerry Allen, with music and acting fit for Broadway.

The PTG has nurtured talent all these years. Think of Rob Winslow and Robert Ainsworth, and now, local playwright and musician Paul Crough with his new play *More than a Memory*, to be staged at the Guild in April.

By developing audiences and a taste for live performance, the Peterborough Theatre Guild has encouraged many groups in our area to thrive: Fourth Line, New Stages, the Gordon Best, the Theatre on King, and Showplace.

But we have to turn off Netflix, and go out.

A Helping Hand with the Law: Community Legal Centre
December 11, 2016

When I was growing up in Kirkland lake, my father, a small-town lawyer, was Legal Director for Timiskaming. I learned early and thoroughly that every person in trouble with the law deserves a defence, one provided by a qualified lawyer. It is an enlightened policy, enshrined in spirit in the Canadian Charter of Rights, Section 7.

But legal fees today are very high. And many people are struggling, especially in Peterborough, to pay rent and find food, heat and transportation.

Not only that, but every aspect of life in a Western bureaucratic state is governed by laws: municipal, provincial and federal. Most of us need a hand navigating these waters, and there be sharks and shoals.

Into the breech comes the Peterborough Community Legal Centre, a friendly and well-run office open for drop-in in visits five mornings a week, and offering free, confidential legal services to low-income people in Peterborough City and County.

Right at the grassroots, downtown at 150 King Street next to the main Post Office, the PCLC occupies four rooms on the fourth floor. It helps people with such matters as Ontario Works, Ontario Disability Support program, rental housing (tenants only), Employment Insurance, workers' rights, consumer protection, and human rights relating to all of these.

There are six staff at the PCLC, with two lawyers, and at the moment, an articling law student. In a creative new program, it also makes use of help from two social workers, realizing that for many people with multiple concerns, support from a professional social worker often enables them to make the presentations and keep the appointments they need.

It is a non-profit agency run by a volunteer board of ten people, who meet monthly. The Chair of the board at present is Dave Nickle. Its is a membership agency with about 80 members, and free to join. I immediately switched from reporter to advocate, and took out a two-year membership. I can now receive the very useful twice yearly newsletter and keep up with all the needs for fairness among vulnerable people on the ground in our city.

Since I have recently become a tenant myself, I browsed the full wall covered with brochures, and discovered that landlords need to issue a 90-day notice if one is to be evicted, and in writing.

Ongoing legal education is important for every citizen today. The PCLC will provide groups with a speaker and other materials. Free public meetings are held, and the Centre is in coalitions with other groups in Peterborough who work on poverty issues. But as Executive Director Melinda Rees says, most people come in as a result of word-of-mouth contact.

When Rees was called to the bar in 1987, she realized she wanted to pursue social justice by working at a community law centre so she started in Belleville, coming to Peterborough in 1991. She feels that helping prevent problems from escalating, work she describes as "at the front end," serves social justice and peace much better than intervening at a crisis point, when damage has been done and criminal courts involved.

Rees also briefs the Ontario government on the effect that laws have "on the ground." For example, in September, the PCLC wrote to the Minister of Labour Kevin Flynn about difficulties with vulnerable workers, and the Employment Standards Act.

The PCLS promotes the legal welfare of low-income residents of Peterborough, a goal well worth pursuing. Ontario has 76 of such legal centres. I have a feeling ours is very responsive and well staffed.

My father would be pleased.

Inspiration Enough in Peterborough
December 22, 2016

These days, in my personal rejection of trumpism, with all its ugly and frightening aspects, I prowl about Peterborough in search of good news stories: stories of people helping one another, respecting others' dignity, building peace and healing. And I find them. They abound.

On December 5, as early dark deepened the feelings of grief experienced by many among us who have said farewell to a loved one this year in death, the locally-owned, non-profit Little Lake Cemetery Company organized its fifth annual Candlelight Memorial gathering.

Though I have a plot in Little Lake ("pre-need," as they say), I didn't know the fascinating history of this public trust, which also owns Highland Park Funeral Centre. I was motivated to read Elwood Jones' wonderful 2010 account, a short book I borrowed from the library, entitled *Little Lake Cemetery: a Public Trust is a Beautiful Thing*.

The Candlelight Service was at Highland Park Funeral Centre on River Road South. It drew nearly 200 people: an open, no-cost, public event where strangers shared mutual sorrow . The room was decorated with giant poinsettias, given by McKnight's Flower Shop. The silence was profound.

In what is becoming a Canadian way of experiencing meditation and finding community without explicit references to the divine, much less making a reference that would exclude any faith or any non-faith, this Candlelight service was unifying, and met a deep need in the community.

I sat beside a burly man who wept silently throughout the half-hour service. With no words, tissue was passed among people, one to another. I spoke to an older woman who said simply, "I have lost everyone. I am alone. This is the first time I have come. I saw it in the newspaper."

David Kennedy, who is a well-respected grief counsellor at Hospice, spoke about memory, and about choosing one's company carefully, people who have given support in the past. He spoke of the importance of including the person's name in holiday gatherings. If tears come, he said, simply tell others you are having a moment of remembrance. His words were entitled "Season's Grievings." Grief, he said is both a necessity and a privilege.

A welcome was offered by Mary McGee, president of Little Lake Cemetery, and a John O'Donohue poem was read by past chair Ann Farlow. Danny Bronson offered his lovely music, instrumental and vocal, with deep feeling and musicianship. Candles were lit. Then there were refreshments, provided by the Cheese Shop.

It was simple, inclusive and gentle, in a gracious space.

My second discovery of goodness was December 6 at Trinity United Church, where Telecare Peterborough held its annual commissioning ceremony for 31 new volunteers. Since 1977, Telecare, which is a free, confidential telephone distress line, one of only five in Canada, has been offering compassionate listening to callers, 24 hours a day, seven days a week. One man has done overnight shifts for 20 years. The Telecare volunteers take 30 hours of training in active listening and knowledge of community services. One young man, a Trent student from Yukon, told me it was the best course he's ever had.

These volunteers seek anonymity. They are known only by their first names. As someone who appreciates publicity, this is a marvel: to do good and no one knows.

For many, it is a dark time, personally and politically. But look "below," not "above," for radiant examples of light, reason and kindness in Peterborough.

Sympathize with the U.S. right now, but resolve to create a different, made-in-Canada ethos. Join the Alberta movement of women so shocked by the "Lock Her Up" chant at a recent Conservative meeting, they formed a "Lift Her Up" campaign.

Merry Christmas.

Anchoring Our Skating Culture
December 29, 2016

Never mind that Auston Matthews, (the Toronto Maple Leafs scoring phenomenon) is from Arizona, we in Peterborough are still an ice-nation writ large.

I saw proof of that this week at Evinrude Seniors Skating.

Five days a week, two hours a day, for $2 (the honour system, drop a toonie in the box), about fifty smooth-gliding older folks, with a ratio of four men to one woman, skate to danceable music, this week's music with a Christmas theme. For me, a rink is the only setting where those hoary tunes are agreeable. No shopping in sight.

And the attire? It is wintery of course, but with ball hats featured, and also lots of helmets. Our city has many fine orthopods and neurologists, but skaters don't want to trouble them unnecessarily at this season. And there is always the question of bone density.

One advantage of seniors' skating at Evinrude is that there are no small people weaving in and out, and stopping sharply to throw skaters off balance. Hand-holding? Just a few, and they are helmeted.

There is of course nothing so sweet as a newly-flooded sheet of ice. Evinrude's is smooth and well-maintained. As coffee break comes, (coffee, 50 cents) there is a flood. The Zamboni comes out as the seniors socialize.

These skaters are organized by Murray Patterson, who is 88, and learned to skate at Inverlea Park in the forties. Being a numbers man, he knows he has covered 65,000 miles of ice over that time.

I approach another smiling couple. She is from Northern Ontario, he from Sherbrooke. They both learned to skate on open-air rinks. Other skaters mentioned their fathers flooding back yards. That still goes on in my neighbourhood, where there are two rinks, both helped along by the City with spigots of water. One surface is for skating, the other for pick-up hockey.

What can be more beautiful than a moonlit evening and silently moving forms against an all-white backdrop?

A woman, originally from Toronto, fondly remembers her backyard rink which surrounded a tree. "That's how I learned to take corners," she laughs. "I stopped skating for 15 years: that was a mistake. There is so much joy in it."

A ruddy-cheeked man tells me he immigrated from the UK to Cape Breton when he was three, and has been skating ever since. Patterson says, "Where else can you get two hours of sport and exercise for two bucks? Not golf!"

One man used one of those skating aids, and another brought his gear in a small, wheeled grocery cart. Most of the women were, like me, in white figure skates with picks, but a few trendy women wore black hockey skates. I don't know how they stop.

The Evinrude skaters had lunch the other day at the Carousel Restaurant. That made me wonder what percentage of our population still skates, with all our hockey leagues, day and night, and our figure skating clubs and outdoor rinks. I know the Syrian refugees are being introduced to the activity.

History tell us the Finns first stated to glide on ice 3000 years ago, with flattened bone attached to the foot. In the 13th century in the Netherlands, steel blades with sharpened edges were attached to boots. Skates then cut into the ice instead of gliding on top.

In the 19th century, Queen Victoria met her future husband Prince Albert while skating. Elegance was valued. I saw traces of that elegance at Evinrude.

Then came "communal games on ice," such as curling, hockey and ringuette. Also, barrel rolling.

In the sense of coming to terms with winter, being at home on ice has its virtues. I'm glad to see that some of my misspent youth as a rink rat at the Kirkland Lake Arena is coming in handy.

Resisting Trumpism in Peterborough
January 5, 2017

I asked readers to tell me how they will cope with trumpism in the next little while. Their responses were so thoughtful, so varied and so wise, I think much of the content should be published as it came.

First of all, I was told by many readers, we in Canada need to recognize how really bad the U.S situation is. "Mr Trump is a narcissist with authoritarian tendencies," said one. There is his dreary and downright frightening list of nominees for cabinet posts. The nominees are hugely rich, far-right, and almost entirely male. They have demonstrated they are unfamiliar with notions of the common good.

We have to be clear-eyed about the dangers and the threat of rule by these people. Here is a doleful run-down by name and position:

Jeff Sessions as Attorney General, is a man so racist he was once refused a judgeship: an enemy of civil rights and women's rights, who has said, "I don't characterize grabbing women by the genitals as sexual assault."

As Treasurer, Steve Mnuchin is an ultra-wealthy former Goldman Sachs executive who foreclosed on 36,000 homes in 2008, in a move a judge called "harsh, repugnant and repulsive."

Secretary of Commerce is Wilbur Ross, a billionaire who has said, "I think the one percent is being picked on for political reasons."

As Environmental Protection administrator, Trump has, deplorably, named Scott Pruitt, who has said climate change is far from settled.

American climate scientists, it is reported reliably, now are going so far as to hide and secure their data secretly to save it from being destroyed, some of it in Canada.

A popular activist site, Avaaz, founded by a Canadian named Ricken Patel, has told the 3 million people who trust its work, that it must move its internet systems out of the U.S. for fear of confiscation.

Education Secretary is to be fundamentalist Betsy de Vos, the Amway heiress, who believes in ending public education in favour of charter schools, and who donated $9 million to the Trump campaign.

As CIA director, Mike Pompeo is a hawkish Tea Party Republican in favour of mass surveillance, who has called for the execution of whistle-blower Edward Snowden.

Secretary of State will be oil magnate with close ties to Russia, Rex Tillerson of Mobil Exxon who is a close friend of Vladimir Putin. They both favour autocracies.

And Defence Secretary Mattis has a nickname: it is "Mad Dog." Nice.

There they are. The fearful quality of the thinking in this group has scholars rushing to re-read Hannah Arendt's 60 year-old-book *The Origins of Totalitarianism*.

As much as the tweeter-president is foolish and shallow, these people are the ones who will make daily life more miserable and more dangerous for the ordinary person. And for us.

Canadians are saying no.

Many say they will absorb this disagreeable information because they live in this world. But no time can be wasted in giving them all "a chance." Collaboration and compromise are not what the times call for. For many, that is not what peacemaking means.

Peterborough Speaks Out
January 12, 2017

Last week's column on resisting trumpism here in Canada described the nightmarish nominations Mr Trump has made for his Cabinet.

Readers have told me what they are going to choose in resistance. A few wrote that they plan to do nothing. They will watch. I have met and must pay respect to Peterburians of the most conscientious kind, who said they have abandoned ship. One professor told me that since election night, he has watched only the Home and Garden channel. A woman wrote that the topic is forbidden in her home: it depresses everyone, especially the teenagers.

But creative ideas from Peterborough people poured in. At the Unitarian Fellowship, poetry is important, especially *The Great Turning* by Christine Fry. At Trent University, 12 social work students led by professor Susan Hillock, will drive to Washington at a cost of $350 each, in a van, to take part in the great Women's March Against Trump's values on January 21, the day after the inauguration. In solidarity, another carload of older women will bus it to Toronto the same day for a similar march at Queens Park, from 12 to 2 pm. Young friends of the students are organizing a fundraiser at The Spill for January 11.

Many correspondents told me they were very disheartened after Trump won the election, and experienced waves of anger, dread and fear. Some are following the advice of Vaclev Havel in Czechoslovakia in the eighties, as he led the anti-Soviet movement to "step out of the lie into the truth." A high school principal wrote: "Our habitat, this beautiful earth, is more important to me that a single individual who may be bent on its destruction, so I will invest my energies to an even greater degree in earth-friendly initiatives."

It was inspiring to see the breadth of people's reading. One young man sent a quote from the Lutheran hero and martyr in the Second World war, Dietrich Bonhoeffer, who died in a concentration camp.

"Stupidity is a more dangerous enemy than malice. One may protest against evil. It can be exposed, but against stupidity we are defenceless. Reason falls on deaf ears."

I wish that I could be in the class of the teacher who sent in four pages of sensible ideas. She is taking a historical perspective. She lists the advances we have made since the thirties: women's rights, civil rights, transition to an acceptance of LGBT people, the fall of the Berlin wall, and the strides in education and health around the world. But she doesn't rest there.

It has been troubling for her. In December, her students told her, "After Trump, life sucks royally." No good teacher leaves the young in that space.

So she culled ideas from Rebecca Solnit, an editor at Harpers magazine, who has written 17 books, among them, *Hope in the Dark*. Solnit says, "Most of the countries in our hemisphere besides Canada, have gone into horror and emerged. But since trumpism is global, we have a responsibility to contain and weaken, and try to defeat trump and trumpism. In easy times, we grow slack."

Hope was generated for this teacher by remembering the cooperative, compassionate and altruistic nature of most humans: she names the Dalai Lama, Karen Armstrong and Dorothy Day. She feels that the obstacles to hope are that students don't have a sense of their own power, nor a sense of belonging. She approves of such initiatives as Peterborough Dialogues and the Art of Hosting.

And as Solnit has said: "We live in a very surprising world."

For the people who analyse economics, these times are ripe with conclusions. One citizen wrote me: "He is just the epitome of a process begun long ago when capitalism became the operating system of most of the world, and has now morphed into global corporatism. By it, all is to be put to the service of profit, and the 15 men who control it."

On another note, a social worker said: "I will find my moral compass and my conscience from First Nations." Proclaimed a wise woman, aged ninety: "We must ask of every issue: does it preserve and protect the natural world unto the seventh generation?"

Ever practical, a musician told me: "I'll donate as best I can to every group that opposes Trump: Planned Parenthood, Black Lives Matter, the Water Protectors. And I'll stay alert to any trumpism rearing its ugly head here in Canada." People know that a brand of such populism is here too.

Another view I received was that "Canadians should focus on issues we face here, not be fixated on big bad trump. Half a million depend on food banks, tens of thousands are living in awful housing conditions. Yes, Trump is a proto-fascist, but we should concentrate on our own country."

A young man teacher wrote to me, "I'm offering a four-week course on feminism to 15-year-olds in 2017. I think it is essential in resisting trumpism." A young man is doing this. I recently read that 65% of women and 35% of men are feminists.

"We will be selling our property in Florida," a woman emailed. "It no longer appeals to us."

And so the thinking and acting around the Trump phenomenon galvanizes our community too.

Trumpery at Work
January 19, 2017

The last two columns expressed how Canadians have experienced the American election of November 8, and how they will cope now.

An international educator wrote: "How am I coping? By trying to understand our times. The neo-liberal order is in decay, but it may be replaced under Trump by something more aggressive. Class has re-emerged as the burning question. Some democratic parties have become parties of capital, hence the rise of authoritarian populism."

139

A 53-year-old woman emailed: "In a nutshell, I am at a complete loss. I continue to focus on quiet meditation and yoga. Since I am a biology teacher, it is clear to me that nature models for us the inclusivity, adaptation and cooperation needed for survival. Trump and his allies should have paid more attention in biology class."

Satiric humour was recommended by many. Quoting Elizabeth Renzetti in the Globe and Mail of December 17, a young mother wrote: "Go ahead, laugh. Humour is a crucial tool in the fight against a surreal upending of democratic norms." Renzetti mentions the biting humour of comics John Oliver, Trevor Noah and Samantha Bee, all immigrants to America.

A thoughtful activist said: "Let's encourage enlightened leaders: NYC mayor Bill de Blasio, California Governor Jerry Brown, and Google CEO Sundar Pichai, all of whom can and will resist trumpism." He spoke of online groups such as Leadnow, WalkFree and SumofUs. "It's a matter of confronting the tweeter-president with some of his own medicine."

Another resident wrote, "People power is one of the only forces strong enough to push back against corrupt politicians and corporations seeking to profit from dividing people, destroying the planet and harming countries."

Richard Heinberg, who writes for a group called *Post Carbon* argues for strong localism as a trump-antidote. He has said, "There will be lots of awful things to oppose and the next four years may be a time when much that is beautiful and admirable about America is attacked, looted, liquidated and suppressed, as some of the more shameful elements of the country are empowered, amplified and celebrated."

But both student and writer agree on the strength of the counter-forces which are mobilizing. There will be a serious economic downturn, they predict. More than one of my respondents spoke of the sense of betrayal coming to Trump voters. "This," says Heinberg, "can lead to national cynicism or to action."

A respected cultural leader in Peterborough told me: "I will be following the time-honoured tradition of artists resisting government through their work in society. My chosen field is theatre, and at the Guild on the last Sunday of each month, there will be an open play-reading of a relevant play. On January 29, it will be about the painter Georgia O'Keefe, in April about the dark side of racism, and in May *Lenin's Embalmers.*"

For me personally, I will wear my "Nasty Woman" T-shirt, whose purchase supported Planned Parenthood, and I will continue to search out these resistance stories for my columns. I am going to the March in Toronto on January 21. I will continue to volunteer with Amnesty International, and donate to local and international causes. I will consult reputable news sources.

Lastly, a neighbour told me lightly, "You know, I've always liked Joe Biden (outgoing VP of the U.S.). As Joe said, we will make lighthouses of ourselves, and shine!"

A Return to Jamaica
January 26, 2017

In Jamaica last week, I had a marriage proposal. Here's how it went.

A smiling man, fortyish, who was dropping his little daughter off for tennis lessons at the convent hostel where I stay in Kingston, paused to chat.

"You are Canadian?" he said.

"Yes."

"Were you born there?" Me, surprised: "Yes, I was."

Pause. "Are you married?" Me, big smile, "Oh yes."

"Oh well then, you can't take me back to Canada."

I really don't think it would have worked out.

I go out on the street every morning at seven to buy a Gleaner newspaper for $60 Jamaican dollars (that's sixty cents Canadian), from the Gleaner lady, Winsome. Many pages today lament the departure of Barack Obama. There are also glowing pictures of fourteen 11-year-olds who are top spellers in their various regions. They are coming to Kingston to compete in the National Spelling Bee. The words they will encounter would stump me, and everyone I know.

We are three women from the Peterborough area: Joyce Mackenzie and Cathie Morrissey to encourage two school projects they support, and me to present my book *Jamaica Journal: the Story of a Grassroots Canadian Aid Organization* to people I have featured in that book.

We are three amigas for sure. Joyce has been a volunteer in this work for forty years, and this time, resisting family trepidation, she rents a car, drives on the left and proceeds into Kingston's teeming inner city, an area without legible street signs and numerous one-way streets. Cathie is serene. One day, when they are lost, a man on a bicycle says, "Follow me!"

Together they labour to bring together the Kingston Rotary Club with teachers to enable a grant to materialize from the Global Fund of Rotary, initiated by Dawn Straka and Paula Wagar of Peterborough. This grant will bring a computer lab to a deprived little school called Tavares Gardens.

I am busy seeing old friends and enjoying their delight as they open the book. Fabian Brown, the consummate community organizer who employed John at no salary in 1998, now works at the Spanish hotel chain Bahia Principe on the North Coast. He is a training manager and works to build the self-esteem of 1700 Jamaican employees. Fabian also ran recently in local elections. He was ahead for awhile, but then his opponent, it was reported, began handing out $15 to voters for their support. Fabian said such a practice demeans the voters, and he refused to do it. He lost by 75 votes.

Angela Stultz, another longtime partner, came by. She now works for the National Housing Trust as a social development officer in a deprived area called Frog City, where people are "outside the system" - paying no tax and pirating electricity and gas. Therefore, they do not qualify for the generous loans for housing which the NHT gives. Angela must bring them in from the cold. If anyone can do it, Angela will.

More adventures. In a shipping container converted to a usable space, we heard a steel pan band rehearse. It was a learning experience: to talk to the all-woman group and see the various pans, sizes and tones. As Raymond Yip Choy of Fleming College will remind me, "Pan is Trinidadian!"

And for Catholics and Anglicans especially, I must mention we participated in an activity in a little baking room off the convent, where Sister Grace Ann makes the communion hosts for the two churches on the whole island. We mixed flour and water and spread the batter on a kind of waffle iron, for one minute of baking at high heat. Then, we punched out the round wafers and bagged them in hundreds, thinking good thoughts of all the people who would be receiving these hosts during services.

Peterborough at the Great March
February 2, 2017

On January 22, I boarded the Greyhound bus at 9 am for the trip to Toronto.

Smiling faces met me: some six or seven women, in pairs, none of them known to me before, headed for the rally. So of course, we chatted, bemoaning the present state of public affairs in the USA, and discussing our footwear and the expected weather.

Why did we take a Saturday for this? Buttons which were handed out to us asked this very question: "Why are you marching?"

There were so many answers and such unity among them. Around me in the Queens Park gardens, I heard:

"To send a signal of support and commiseration to my American sisters, in what they have to face now."

"To give hope to my daughters."

"To say NO loud and clear to all this man stands for."

"To join what looks like a huge global march for decent values."

"I've never been at a protest but it's time. Women have been so insulted."

None of us could have imagined what was to come for us this day: participating in a one-million person action around the world, on seven continents, including 600 cities and towns, 30 of them in Canada: in Australia and on a science boat in Antarctica (the "Penguins for Peace").

In Oslo, Rome, Paris, London, Amsterdam, Madrid, Seoul, Tokyo. If this is the age of information, bring it on. My companion Janice had her excellent sign mounted on a wire frame "Feminism Trumps Trump!"

I managed a few photos with my iPad, and met delightful people, young and old. We "Nasty Women" types met each other and hugged. A little girl nearby, about 8, carried a sign proclaiming "Canada is already great." Her older sister's said "Future Nasty Woman!" It seemed every second person had taken the creative trouble to make a sign. That of one man said: "Gloria Steinem is my hero."

Another said "You can't comb over sexism." The signs were witty, clever and sarcastic, but there was no note of hate. It was a release, a lifting of the funk that has engulfed millions of people since the result of that weird and even illegitimate election November 8.

More signs to cheer: "We shall overcomb!" And this one: "Super callous fascist racist extra braggadocius!" Try saying that one.

Or, "I didn't come from your rib, you came from my vagina." And over there: "Now you've p—d-off grandma!"

To put one's body out on the street involves a very small bit of risk, but the growing crowd was good-natured, even exuberant: not a police person in sight. I've heard the Toronto walk drew 60,000 people. I'd say 20% were men.

It was also the strengthening of the "Build a Hedge" movement, a smart and positive effort to join with other Canadians in asserting we must not go there: to this new age of toxic racism and misogyny.

It was led by, and organized by women, but it wasn't solely women's causes: all the well-known Trump targets were supported in the speeches.

One thing I noticed with joy: of the six splendid orators gearing us up to walk to City Hall, five were women of colour: Indigenous, Asian, brown and black. This being Toronto, this being Canada, it was not even remarked on. I saw through tears in my eyes Adrienne Clarkson and Margaret Atwood, arm-in-arm.

I noticed that good financial support had come from the union, UNIFOR. Their members should be proud.

Then Janice reminded me that Sandi, from our Trent fitness class, had given her a generous amount of money to treat ourselves to a drink and supper. It was enough to include three other new friends.

And we got thumbs-up all around.

New Words Help Us Think
February 9, 2017

Like you, I'm trying, trying, to understand this world we are living in.

I read. I listen. I discuss. I go to art exhibits and film festivals. I debate with my brother. I drink red wine. I'm getting up at 5 am, reaching for my iPad.

And as an old English teacher, I believe we need words, sometimes new words, with which to think. The thinking cannot happen without the words.

So when I discovered three new words this week that threw some light on my confusions, I grasped them with delight.

First of all, American novelist Philip Roth, who is now 83, told the New Yorker magazine his opinion of Mr Trump in no uncertain words.

"He is ignorant of government, of history, of science, of philosophy, of art and destitute of decency. He is incapable of recognizing nuance and has a vocabulary of seventy-seven words."

Now that's a powerful wielding of words that conveys meaning. But new words?

"Almond" is the first.

Entering the debate which followed the women's march and what it meant or might lead to, we were full of self-congratulation, until we started to see the critiques leveled by black women. One sign said: "We black women are again cleaning up white women's mess."

What it pointed to was the fact that Mr Trump was really elected by white women's votes, not the votes of black or Hispanic women. Fifty percent of white women voted for him. Until that blessed day when we are all colour-blind, we will be thinking and speaking about colour.

On the weekend, I heard a new word which I think can be helpful. It describes the colour of skin of an Arab or Muslim woman. It is "almond," and the term was offered to me by a Muslim friend in the Nexicom Lounge of Showplace during a coffee break at Reframe Film Festival.

That lounge was an ongoing forum for deep discussion, and there was great food too, from By the Bridge and Silk Roots Fusion Cuisine.

I was telling my friend how happy I was, that the Toronto March had been led by women of colour.

"What colour?" she asked.

"Indigenous, black, brown and Asian," I answered.

"Well," she said with a smile, "We Muslims from the Middle East are just beginning to describe ourselves as 'almond.' "

Got it! Lovely. "Almond."

Then there has been the puzzle of the loaded word "Christian" in political discourse. How can those men in the White House, the Paul Ryans and Mike Pences and the Steve Bannons of the world, all self-described Catholics, even the newly-saved Donald Trump, call themselves "Christian" as they pour forth dark and harmful policies? Walls and bans and attacks on the press and the trampling of women's rights, and the gutting of the environmental protection agency?

Here, Pope Francis has been of some help. He said this week, "It is hypocritical to call yourself Christian without practising the beatitudes. The sickness Jesus condemns most is hypocrisy."

Keep talking, Pope.

Again, new word time: it is "Christo-fascist." For some commentators, the term is "Christianists." Frauds. It could describe the evangelical right-wing and the white fundamentalist Protestants.

Calling out to their God and harming everyone else. The appropriation of a term to identify oneself doesn't really mean a thing. One's actions do the identification.

So there are two more useful words that bring some clarity to the situation down south. I plan to adopt and use those words when I observe, judge and act.

STOP THE PRESS: my friend Craig Paterson has supplied a crucial fourth word, if we can get our tongues around it.

It is "kakistocracy," first uttered in 1829, and it means a state or country run by the worst, least qualified and most unscrupulous citizens.

Case rests.

The Daily Newspaper Struggles
February 16, 2017

Nobody put me up to this column on the plight of newspapers in Canada today. And, of course I make my fortune writing for this one every week.

But the state they are in, concerns me very much. It must concern everyone.

The daily newspaper has been around for almost 200 years, the lifeblood of a community. It is a proud carrier of news and information, creating a well-informed and involved body of citizens, who speak and organize and influence public opinion and policy.

The story of Canadian newspapers is a fascinating one. It involved heroes, and still does, today.

Consider this: *The Peterborough Examiner* has five staff in the editorial department. Five, where once it had 22. All young, smart and hard working. The honour and the burden of journalism.

The printing press was invented 500 years ago. Newspapers started as gazettes, printed and controlled by governments in the early 1800's. Then editors began campaigns to assert independence and make room for political opinion of all stripes, largely, at that time, about our moving to responsible government from colonial status.

For Peterborough, it all started in 1847. That's a lot of years of service. We had the glory days of Robertson Davies, famous novelist, who wrote editorials limited to 3 paragraphs. He led from 1942-1955, and was followed by Ralph Hancox, who went on to edit *Readers Digest*, and whose daughter Linda now teaches at Adam Scott Collegiate.

The Examiner logo was designed by award-winning artist, the late David Bierk.

Then came the time national chains began to acquire community newspapers. The problem of concentration reared its head. *The Examiner* was sold to the Thomson Chain. It is now owned by Postmedia Corp. (CEO Paul Godfey; over 50 newspapers; 4700 employees, based in Toronto; 35% foreign-owned, shares at 90 cents today).

The struggle is to keep local voices in the mix, while publishing required columns sent by head office.

My *Examiner* is now 20 pages. I like the quiet thump as it lands on my balcony. I now pay online three months at a time for $55, and add a good tip for the carrier. A confession: I can't understand why so many of my Peterborough friends do not receive the print edition and pay this modest amount. They insist that they go online. But it ain't the same as a sit-down with the paper and a cup of coffee.

I pick up at random an *Examiner*, February 6. I learn about City Council topics. I read about a great idea, not paving driveways. I look with relief at the obits. No one I know today. I admire the Polar Plungers. I read my horoscope, always the possibility of romance. And the pictures. Cliff Skarstedt is a genius.

The Examiner prints only 12,000 hard copies a day. That is a disabling disgrace in a region of 130,00 people. Of course, the paper gets 1 million hits a month on its site. People want to keep up with this community.

But it's bleeding red ink.

Editors tell me one big mistake was committed in the 90's when newspapers gave away content, the intellectual and investigative treasure now taken for granted.

What can help? Readers who understand the dilemmas and will pay regularly for its work, for one. Maybe government support. CBC gets some. This is democracy we are talking about. The closing of tax loopholes is another, so that advertisers choose Canadian media in which to advertise, not American ones.

In an important new report called *The Shattered Mirror: News, Democracy and Trust in the Digital Age*, veteran journo Ed Greenspon expresses some simple truths (not alternative facts). *The Toronto Star* commented:

"Canada matters, journalists matter, original civic news matters, freedom of the press matters, digital innovation matters, diversity of voices matters and financial sustainability matters."

We must value and strengthen the local press.

Crossing to the U.S.A.
February 23, 2017

It certainly won't be with the same trepidation as that felt by 22 refugees from Djibouti who walked across frozen fields for 12 kilometres to Emerson, Manitoba (population 650) two weeks ago from North Dakota, enduring minus 20 degrees cold, and not feeling their feet, until picked up by the RCMP and taken to a refugee claimant centre.

There they had bread and Nutella, and slept on the floor of a community centre.

But it was with a little bit of trepidation that I approached the U.S. border a week ago, carrying with me, not Muslim prayers in my I-phone, but my book, *Psalms for Everyday*, all my anti-trumpism Examiner columns on my laptop, and an eerie sense of dread.

At Pearson airport, customs seemed more extensive than previously, and one's picture is taken, but the personal interview is brief: address in the States and return date to Canada.

In this age of uncertainty, when university professors are declining to go to academic conferences in America as a protest against the "Muslim ban," a relative of mine counsels me not to go either, in solidarity with banned people. I have solicited advice before making a decision. The result of 40 informal responses to my question by friends and acquaintances, including a discussion with thoughtful Trent students at their annual Community Conference on February 4, was about fifty-fifty. One young man from Malaysia was eloquent about my need to go: continue friendships, he said, offer encouragement to the resisters and play a role in history!

A favorite teacher friend urged: "Look, I can go to PEI instead of Cape Cod and to Montreal instead of New York." Yep.

What have I found here? It is Arizona. As expected, ordinary lives are lived without drama. Arizona has 6 million people; 80% of whom are white Americans. In the winter, there are 900,000 Canadian snowbirds, most from the western provinces. I speak with many more Trump supporters than I have ever encountered.

Someone gives me a copy of the largest newspaper, the Arizona Republic. It is a liberal paper! It devotes two separate articles to fact-checking what is coming from the White House.

It reports on protests for and against Planned Parenthood. It predicts that a motion to make Phoenix a sanctuary city is bound to fail. I notice that the term "left" is widely used to describe progressive positions. "Left" in many circles here is derogatory.

I play Trivial Pursuit in a bar with a couple from Iowa: he voted Clinton, she, Trump. Our team is second in the game, acing the question on the novel *1984*, but missing out on Diana Ross' two last hits.

The Arizona Republic prints a long story on the successful growing of green leafy vegetables out near Yuma, which supplies the US, Canada and Mexico during the months of October and March each year, by bringing Mexican farm workers over each day for harvesting.

I am able to do my morning aquafit to a CD in the open air and relish a grapefruit that tastes as it should. But then I am shocked to see ads for private ultrasound testing by a for-profit outfit called "HealthFair." "$137 for seven heart and artery tests that are "consumer-driven and free from government intervention."

Actually, 700,000 Arizonans would lose health coverage if the Affordable Care Act is repealed.

Hundreds of people have just shown up at a mosque to show support for Muslim Americans. Phoenix has the world-famous Heard Museum of Native Art and Culture, with a stunning new exhibit, "Beauty Speaks For Us."

This dark time will pass, I am encouraged to think. But we are going to have to be like Finland, thriving, while dramatically different from our next-door neighbours.

Peterborough Singers Honour Women
March 2, 2017

Last week I was musing on how we Canadians must now, thoughtfully and assertively, create and strengthen our cultural and political reality in the next little while to counter what is happening to America.

And then on Saturday, I witnessed a stunning and unexpected demonstration of this very thing.

Out of local talent that is second to none anywhere in this country, and from a gem of an idea from my esteemed fellow columnist David Goyette, came a program of music that celebrated Canadian women, Canadian life, in a way I have never seen.

Carried to fulfillment by the brilliant husband and wife duo of Syd and Pam Birrell and the 100 trained voices of the Peterborough Singers, the concert, called *Canadian Women in Song* enthralled some 900 attendees at Calvary Church.

Syd is a gifted classical conductor, who will now turn to Mozart for the May 6 *Requiem Mass* performance here in Peterborough. But as a partner to the vibrant Pam, who asked him to arrange the mostly pop songs which Canadian women have successfully sung over the past 50 years, he entered into long research assisted by his teenage daughter, and rose to write beautiful arrangements for the voices. Steve McCracken did the band arrangements. Syd modestly said he was happy to just sing along this concert, leaving the conducting to Pam, which she did with joy and verve.

What concert-goers took away was a huge admiration for the collaboration it all showed. What could be more appropriate for International Women's Day, March 8, than this performance? It deserves national coverage. Suitably, it was attended by Canada's Minister for the Status of Women, Maryam Monsef.

So whose songs would you expect to hear in such a program? The planners had the dilemma of selecting fifteen singer/composers, out of hundreds that came to mind, and they apologized in advance for leaving out some great work (i.e. Diana Krall, Molly Jackson, Amy Sky).

But we heard memorable renditions of songs made popular by Susan Aglukark, Anne Murray, Sylvia Tyson, Rita MacNeil. K.D. Lang, Joni Mitchell, Jann Arden, Sarah McLaughlin, Lesley Feist, Carly Rae Jepson, Avril Lavigne, Serena Ryder, Celine Dion and Shania Twain. As the concert had begun with an Indigenous artist, it ended with Buffy Ste. Marie.

Linda Kash humorously gave the audience a bit of biographical information about each woman as the concert proceeded. Small towns in Alberta seems to have produced the most!

This concert had none of the flag-waving fervour so often seen in our southern neighbours, but it hummed with a quiet patriotism and pride in real accomplishment and creativity. Joni Mitchell is a true poet and philosopher, one realizes.

It was also an expansion in everyone's musical experience. Certainly expanded mine. Did I ever really hear, let alone enjoy, the lyric of Stompa until Saturday? The Peterborough Singers are nurturing young talent, and 12 of them sang some contemporary favorites with gusto. Did you really know that the spirit of *Call Me Maybe* is poignant and uncertain?

The concert featured a highly professional back-up band with Rob Phillips, Barry Haggerty, Curtis Cronkwright, Andrew Affleck and David Goyette (the man is everywhere). The soloists were radiant: Kate Suhr, Victoria Pearce and nineteen-year-old Tanya-Leah Watts.

One of the blessings of living here for so many years is that I know so many people in this group of singers. I taught at St Peter's with Mary Claire Nepotiuk. The Unitarians are there big time: Marion Habermehl, Ben Wolfe and Jovanna Soligo. Barb and Rick Hilts lead service at the Mount. Fred Huffman and Walter Downes are neighbours. Andy and Erinn Burke, brother and sister, are involved in international work.

For me, it's not going too far to say Calvary Church was holy ground last Saturday.

GSA Groups Increase Safety and Inclusion
March 10, 2017

One day last week, former Peterborough Roman Catholic bishop William McGrattan, now gone to Calgary, said that while he may choose softer language than his predecessor, Bishop Fred Henry, who was famous for hard lines on sexual matters, his views that are not different.

Bishop McGrattan is opposed to Gay-Straight Alliances in high schools, "since they promote a certain lifestyle," and he doesn't "believe in categorizing young people."

That very day I attended a Gay-Straight Alliance meeting at a local Catholic high school. I wish the bishop had been with me at St. Peter. I think he would have been re-assured, to say nothing of edified at the interactions among 50 or so conscientious students who are taking seriously their mission to support one another.

In 2012, then Education Minister Laurel Broten amended the Education Act to strengthen its anti-bullying section. It requires that publicly-funded schools in this province offer help to students who want to organize a Gay-Straight Alliance, if even one student requests it. The clubs are to be advised by a teacher, and called "Gay-Straight Alliances," not "Equity Clubs" or "Respecting Differences" clubs. Because, as Broten pointed out, problems need to be named before change can happen.

That was almost five years ago. The Toronto Public School Board now proudly proclaims that 60 of its secondary schools have GSAs. The Canadian Civil Liberties Association hails the difference such clubs make in the overall welcoming climate of the school. Teachers everywhere overwhelmingly say school morale rises, inclusion increases and mood improves.

The 2012 policy change in Queen's Park was supported by the teachers' union, the Ontario English Catholic Teachers Association, a huge boost. But the Catholic Trustees Association objected. At times teachers, who are daily in touch with the young, differ from publicly elected trustees who are to mind the finances, and are often torn between their perceived duty to uphold "Catholic teaching" as they understand it, and the needs of their students.

The fact is that teenagers often hear remarks in their classes: "That's so gay," and other insulting terms. Cyber-bullying has emerged as an issue for vulnerable teens.

Meanwhile here in Peterborough at St. Peter Secondary School, the head of English, who is a widely-respected teacher-mentor, Joe Webster, said he would be the teacher-advisor. He has found it deeply rewarding work for justice. The club meets once a week over lunch. I was privileged to attend my second GSA meeting this week.

The knowledge, sophistication and kindness of these youth was very impressive. The kids come, munching their lunches in a comfortable atmosphere, as they offer insightful analysis of the current situation. A few of the students are gay, I would think: most are straight. It doesn't seem to matter.

Today's meeting seems to focus on what transgender means, and what being an ally means. At a previous meeting, some youth wept openly as they discussed the targeted shooting of LGBT people at an Orlando club. They follow the news closely: worry about Trump's America, discuss sports and sexual identity.

The teacher-librarian, Shelley Hughes, quotes from a hero during the Nazi era, Rev Martin Niemoller, who said famously: "First they came for the communists, but I wasn't a communist......so I did nothing. (then they came for other categories: Jews, gypsies, homosexuals). When they came for me, there was no one left to help."

Science teacher Helen Lynett offers a few matter-of-fact realities about transgender biology. Webster, these teachers and others are doing crucial work, closely tied to their vocation as leaders.

Most of the discussion is offered by the students. And they leave cheerful, stronger, more knowing, and accepting of all. They'll be back next week, learning again how to advocate for others.

Perhaps, that's what schools should be accomplishing?

Nordic Skiing: Beloved in the Kawarthas
March 16, 2017

There is a sport widely practised in the Kawarthas, and all throughout Ontario, that generally flies under the radar of public consciousness. But it has hundreds of passionate practitioners, supporters and volunteers, with some 25 clubs operating in Ontario, many in the northern parts.

Its combines a dazzling degree of physical fitness and endurance among its elite participants, similar I'd say to the cardiac condition of a diver or a rower.

It has the great and under-rated advantage of being outdoors. Once, we Canadians were more an outdoor people. Before cities and highways, we lived more in tune with the outdoors. Maybe we talked about it less. But now, with X-country, there is bliss: no loud gyms, sweaty smells, body contact, expensive gear, or roar of the crowd. On some trails, there is no sound at all except bird song, and no company other than the curious glance of a rabbit, a fox or a small deer.

There is a vulnerability to the elements, and an attitude of acceptance, a philosophical surrender of control, along with a finely-tuned sense of the temperature and the conditions. And knowledge of waxing.

Fast-growing in the Kawarthas today is the Nordic Ski Club. It has a well-maintained website (*www.kawathanordic.ca*) telling skiers how many kilometres up at the club near Haultain, north of Young's Point, are ready for skiing. It's been a good winter. The club membership is nearing 900 persons, mostly young families, and it has hosted two major tournaments: the COSAA championships for high school athletes and the provincial midget races, age 10-14 last weekend.

I was struck by the cheeriness, the scores of volunteers, the 200 young skiers in their numbered bibs on their 5 km run, the bilingual public address announcements, and the ringing bells to start. To say nothing of the beauty of glistening snow and a wide blue sky.

People in the rental shop explained the features of classic skiing (42 km available) and skate skiing (27 km available). There is snowshoeing (10 km) and night skiing. The rates are very reasonable: a season pass for a family is $205, for an adult $126, a senior $120 and a student $65.

Kawartha Nordic hires four part-time workers: a groomer, a rental manager, a youth program co-ordinator, and a leader of instruction. It is run by a board of volunteers.

I remember days in the seventies when these late gentlemen, Tom Bennet, Don Mackenzie and Doug Tanney devoted hours to cutting and grooming trails, all without modern equipment.

Its fans speak in almost mystical terms of the sense of peace and well-being they experience, skiing quietly along a trail of white on a sunny day. We may not catch up to the Scandinavians, but we have a creditable record of achievement, and many KN youth go on to college programs.

I chatted with two of the dedicated KN leaders, Bruce Wurtele and Kent Todd. The volunteer board manages a budget of about $40,000 annually. It receives some grants from the Trillium Foundation and from local sponsors such as Champlain Animal Hospital, Wild Rock Outfitters, and LLF Lawyers.

I spoke with a mother from Parry Sound who told me her family had started skiing early. All members can take part and travel together. I asked one young lad what a "buff" was. He was very informative. There are classes on weekends for kids, taught mostly by volunteers. I would not be a jackrabbit and I'm not a master with experience, so I guess I'm an adult beginner.

In terms of wholesomeness, I'd rate cross-country skiing up there with Sunday dinner or Christmas eve. We're lucky to have so many participants in our area, building community and a connection with creation.

Teenager on Parliament Hill
March 23, 2017

I had arranged to meet fifteen-year-old Kaia Douglas at a coffee shop downtown. I watched her pull up on her bike (it was minus 15 degrees), the bike with flowers on the handlebars, hop off and come in to greet me, with her level intelligent gaze.

Then she ordered a Nanaimo bar and we sat down to chat.

Kaia, a drama student at TASS, left me breathless when she described her activities. At TASS, in addition to drama courses, she is taking English, math, history, science and civics-and-careers. That is the beginning. She plays hockey, both for the school and for the city "Icekats," and "sometimes referees." She cross-country skis out at the Nordic club.

An environmentalist, she tells me that she and her friends were very disheartened after the Trump election. One thing they did was reach out to older women for advice on staying the course and finding hope. More than one woman responded.

In the meantime. Kaia is directing a play called *Captain Bree and Her Lady Pirates*, a musical for St James Players to be staged at the end of April. The cast numbers 26 young people, many near her age.

She has just spent March 8, International Women's Day, on Parliament Hill, invited to shadow Hon Maryam Monsef, Minister for the Status of Women, as she made three major speeches around Ottawa that day. Kaia's dad drove her over and she has a grandmother to stay with in Ottawa.

It was a whirlwind day, beginning with the annual IWD breakfast at City Hall hosted by Mayor Jim Watson. Monsef asked the 200 attendees to find a young woman and mentor her, as she realizes her potential.

Then it was on to Centre Block for a tour of the parliament buildings. Kaia was dazzled by the National Library and the marble halls with their dramatic sculptures.

To her delight, a feminist NGO called Equal Voice had arranged to bring to Ottawa 338 young women ages 18-23, for four days of intensive workshops on leadership and political participation. The project was capped off by the young women taking seats in the House of Commons in the places ordinarily occupied by their federal MP's. Thirty one-minute speeches were made, highlighting the concerns of the young women, especially in their districts.

The young delegates had applied several months previously, and Equal Voice made the selection. Peterborough-Kawartha was represented by Hillary Scanlon, a student at Wilfrid Laurier University in Kitchener-Waterloo. The enterprise was called "Daughters of the Vote." I looked at the 338 faces online. Total diversity, expressing Canada today.

Kaia heard Monsef and Sophie Gregoire-Trudeau speak to this group, and she met many of them. Then, in Part 3 she attended a reception in the lobby of the National Arts Centre and had yet another chance to hear the Minister's remarks. Canada's Parliament is just 26% female, and in that category, ranks 46th in the world.

Kaia brought me up-to-date with renovations to the Parliament Buildings. Some have called the three blocks the handsomest parliament in the world. They have needed extensive reinforcing, including "seismic upgrades" (that's for earthquakes), electrical repairs, stonework and a new roof. This is estimated to cost $3 billion over ten years. While the Centre Block which houses the House of Commons is being renovated, Parliament will sit in the West Block in a former courtyard covered by a glass roof to become usable space. The move will be done next year.

I asked Kaia how the experience left her feeling. "More hopeful," she said, "more excited about possibilities in the future."

At the same time, she has caution well beyond her years, as she both participates, and watches "how it will all roll out."

The Mount, John Martyn, and Housing
March 30, 2017

One cannot think of social housing in Peterborough without John Martyn's name leaping to mind.

The retired teacher and theatre director, now a member of the Pathway of Fame with his spouse Nora, John has toiled effectively and persistently in the field of affordable housing in Peterborough for over 25 years.

He has been, all this time, a volunteer. He was convinced early in his life that real progress for individuals and families is largely based on their having a safe, secure place to live, ideally costing just 30% of their income. But with low levels of both social assistance and minimum wage, this is a still-distant goal. John, who was always drawn to social justice work, set out to do something about it, which culminated in the exciting 2017 development of the Mount Community Centre.

"It is going gangbusters," he smiles.

The long-time convent of the Sisters of St. Joseph had been sold to a Calgary developer in 2009 and then left empty for some years, until a community board purchased it in 2013 with financial help from three levels of government: the Community Foundation, private donors and corporations.

Designed to be a community hub, with affordable housing of 43 units (seven adapted for the disabled), along with commercial and office space for rent, several public spaces, a Gothic chapel, a Gathering Space and an auditorium, the historic landmark has 133,000 square feet of space. "It is perfect for events and the performing arts," John says.

In fact, the Peterborough Youth Choir and the Youth Orchestra are now using the Mount. There are currently two tenants: the VON and Kawartha Land Trust.

The Centre occupies 10 acres of prime, city-centre land, each year growing in value. There is interest in its tree canopy from the Forest Management Course at Fleming College, and from Trent University. Students come to do research.

The manager is Andi van Koeverden. The Mount has a board of ten members, chaired by lawyer Steve Kylie. The Annual General meeting, with audit reports, is held in April. Its website is *www.themountpeterborough.ca.*

John, who is nearing 80 years of age, was born and raised in Peterborough. He remembers going on Saturday mornings to the Public Library to Children's Story Time led by Miss Wesley. He did a lot of reading. His home had the ten-volume set *Journeys through Bookland.*

His family was active in Sacred Heart Parish, and he attended the University of Toronto, then taught in Elliot Lake, where poverty had a strong impact on his decisions.

"Literature, especially Canadian, has always had a big place in my life," he says. "I am a Christian with a Catholic background, but hardly traditional!"

Why this activism at this age? "I don't play golf," John laughs, "I am in reasonable health. I don't know one end of a hammer from another! I was influenced by poet Dennis Lee's collection *Civil Elegies* in which he writes: 'to furnish, out of the traffic and smog and the shambles of dead precursors, a civil habitation that is human and our own.' "

The goal of Peterborough's 10-year Housing Plan is 500 units, and the Mount hopes to contribute 65 units. "We start major construction in May."

Sister Joyce Murray, CSJ who has a doctorate in social justice theology, told me that when she returns home at night and sees lights on, her heart soars. In a warm touch, Sr Joan Driscoll CSJ, an ardent supporter of the project, has moved into one of the apartments. "I want to be among the people," she says.

"It's hard work," John says. "There is disappointment, and no pats on the back, but you look at it through another lens, through what you hope is social good."

A Model for the Young: Hillary Scanlon April 6, 2017

This week, yet another story about an impressive young Peterborough woman gaining notice in Ottawa: in this case, Hillary Scanlon, a 22-year-old St. Peter's graduate, now studying at Wilfrid Laurier University in Kitchener-Waterloo. Hillary just spent the week of a lifetime in Ottawa-Hull, selected to represent the Peterborough-Kawartha riding in a one-week leadership, development, and practical politics conference organized by the non-government group "Equal Voice."

The ambition of Equal Voice is that young women leaders become familiar with Canada's political institutions, and the men and women serving in them, so they will be equipped and inspired to participate in the formal sphere in the years to come. Their first-ever course was called *Daughters of the Vote*.

Equal Voice, led by Nancy Peckford, found the sponsors and the funds to bring 338 young women between the ages of 18 and 23, one from each federal riding, to Ottawa to represent their community and communicate their vision for Canada.

Hillary first heard of the opportunity from her uncle in Ottawa. She applied nine months ago, and heard in December she had been chosen. She had been an active high school student, and member of the model United Nations and other social justice groups. She was a leader in inclusion practices, teacher Bernadette Peters remembers.

Hillary entered university strong in science and math, but took a year of general studies, something she highly recommends. By the end of the year, she switched to Global Studies and Arabic, with a minor in social entrepreneurship. In Ottawa, Hillary found it easy to make friends as the week went on. She met many Indigenous young women. "It was amazingly diverse," she says.

There was a march from the National Arts Centre to Parliament Hill, and a signature song entitled *Strong Women*.

163

She also chuckles when telling me that she had never been to the House of Commons before, having missed the school trip in grade 10 in favour of playing OFSAA field hockey.

The young women sat in the House on March 8, questioned the Prime Minister, and gave thirty one-minute speeches. A powerful and poignant note is that Hillary has recently been losing her eyesight. With courage and determination, she has made adjustments, and continues to achieve. Her family, friends and the university have been very supportive and accommodating. Technically, she scans her textbooks in to a device which renders the text available on audio recording. She works to increase public awareness and erase stigma associated with vision loss, working with a campus group called "Eye to Eye." Hillary says modestly that her participation in this program in Ottawa encouraged the organizers to make adaptations. "We all learned things," she said laughing.

In 1916, some provinces granted women the right to vote in provincial elections. It would take another 45 years for all women over the age of 18, including Indigenous women on reserves, to win the right to vote at every level.

26% of the members of the federal House are now women. To Hillary's chagrin, however, a majority of Canadians said in a recent poll that "the right number" or "too many" women are in political leadership.

Hillary's commitment is to go back to her community and educate. She can be invited to speak to groups and schools by contacting info@equalvoice.ca.

In a little-reported incident, when Daughters of the Vote were in the House of Commons, a delegate making a speech, who also has a disability, had trouble speaking. Hillary moved out of her seat and went to her side. This was reported to MP Maryam Monsef by an admiring Speaker, Geoff Regan.

Does Hillary consider herself a feminist. "Absolutely. The term is no longer negative. It has been normalized."

An emerging leader indeed.

Bus Ads Reveal Weaknesses in Council
April 13, 2017

In future, friends, never vote for a municipal politician, or any politician really, who cannot show he/she has taken and passed a women's studies course.

The present display of ugly anti-choice bus ads that demean women, intrude on personal decision-making, induce guilt and shame, and make our public spaces mean-spirited, is on our buses for the next three distasteful months.

Our leadership did not consult the best legal advice, which had been sent to them by people who specialize in women's health and rights. A City Councillor, (disclosure: I ran and lost, in 2010) cannot be expected to know everything about every issue, but their insensitivity to this one, and their blindness to our current culture and its values is profound.

Now there are lame attempts to say "sorry." There are suggestions that the money earned ($1800) go to a women's shelter. There is the publishing of a telephone number so that citizens can object to the ads. There is a promise to do better. It all seems to me late and weak.

Just how many Peterburians, particularly the vulnerable among us, have been hurt and distressed? One woman, a mother of an eight-year-old, said to me, "I had seen these ads online in advance, but the lurid giant lettering gutted me completely."

Spokespeople, in official responses, speak of their "being bound by the principle of freedom of speech." A little deeper investigation into precedents would have revealed that the Charter does not protect hate speech or speech that does harm.

In Grande Prairie, Alberta, in the Court of Queen's Bench last December, Mme Justice C.S. Anderson ruled that indeed the city had the right to refuse the same ads as we have now, on the grounds that they contravene section 14 of the Advertising Code against "unacceptable depictions and portrayals," and would create "a hostile environment for transit users and other uses of the road."

Properly presented, it's not rocket science, the law. City Council was told months ago that they could safely refuse these ads. Information was presented repeatedly by letter and email and personal lobby. Local activists were strengthened by the involvement of the Abortion Rights Coalition of Canada in Vancouver, and its impressive Executive Director, Joyce Arthur.

Arthur will join a public discussion at Sadleir House on April 30.

"Stop the Killing" the ads say. Killing? Doctors, who perform about 300 abortions year at PRHC, mostly for distraught 14 to 19-year-olds, are killers? Women are murderers?

Abortion numbers across Canada are going down gradually each year, with the rise of women's self-esteem and their knowledge of contraception. No thanks to the propaganda work of the Canadian Centre for Bio-Ethical Reform.

Not only has the tone of our city been lowered, but we are a national embarrassment again (no, not a plane landing on Lansdowne Street or a terrible fire-bombing of a mosque), but something very serious.

In a recent case, a leader sought advice on a topic he was urgently concerned about: the fate of the earth. Pope Francis in 2016 said to his Lutheran scientist-friend Prof. Hans Schnellnhuber: "Tell me everything I need to know about climate change." Then he went on to write a widely-hailed letter, *Laudato Si: On Care for Our Common Home*.

Casey Remy Summers, one of the leaders in the women's resistance to the ads, has made a list of suggestions to the City. Apologize for the harm done. Release information on what will be done with feedback received from the public. Link the city site to the site of the Advertising Standards Council of Canada site where more objections can be filed. Inform people of the city's transit policy.

But for now, Peterborough has been outsmarted, outflanked and outraged. There must be a lesson here.

Canada at 150 Years of Age
April 20, 2017

What are you doing to mark Canada 150?

One starts, I think, with a slowly-dawning realization that this year, 2017, will be acknowledged in most quarters with joy and gratitude, but that it is not a cause for celebration among Canada's Indigenous people.

The commemorations should take note of that reality. Our country has a deep, dark side of its past. We from the dominant culture, must hold that truth, too. The dark and the light co-exist.

I recently saw a troubling statistic: Canada's white women are in 6th place among all the world's countries for their well-being. Canada's native women place 63rd on that scale.

This must haunt us all. Let the Inquiry into Missing and Murdered Indigenous Women and Girls soon to start, throw light on all the causes of a dreadful Canadian statistic. And on the solutions.

Even our individual and neighbourhood commemorations can begin with acknowledgement of the pain and bad policies that damaged the original group on the land.

We are three months in to this significant anniversary year now, and marvellous creative ideas keep cropping up, which I hear about as I go around.

Some friends are going to Manitoba to walk a part of the trans-Canada Trail. It is complete now. Another woman told me she is asking her husband to dig up the front lawn and plant a vegetable garden. A grandmother is taping, (I believe it is called PVR'ing), the whole series *Anne,* a poignant new eight-hour production on CBC TV.

My street is planning a June Canada 150 BBQ, to begin with the singing of the national anthem in both languages, then burgers, and a quiz on Canadiana. A man told me he is going to climb the CN Tower.

Another is going to "learn, really learn" 10 new bird species. A book club member is reading all five "Canada Reads" titles, even if it takes a year. Another friend is paddling for the first time in the Dragon Boat races in June. Whoever said we Canadians were a sedentary bunch?

Our cultural institutions beckon. Who's in for the National Ballet-created dance, which we can all dance together in a public space, because it's simple choreography? There are instructional videos on the National Ballet site. We're certainly going to try it on Manning Avenue in June. First step: slap the wall on one side and then on the other.

I vividly remember Expo 67, when the country was 100 years old. That's fifty years ago. It turned out to be an exuberant, six-month-long celebration of us. I was living in Dorval, Quebec in a bungalow at the time, with a husband and two small kids, and I had been a skeptic for months. All that mud being moved to make a site, I scoffed. And a dome! Who was Buckminster Fuller anyway? Those national pavilions: just promoting their own commerce. Plus, where was one to park?

I was dead wrong about our centennial exhibition. It shaped and encouraged us. We cheered about this country. It had francophone flourish and fun. The Expo site had quality day-care, costing a pittance. I had fiddleheads for the first time, and Arctic char. My spouse found a hidden parking place under a bridge somewhere, and delighted in showing all our visitors around. We had season-long passports.

This time, no Bobby Gimby singalong, but the Toronto Symphony (*www.canadamosaic.tso.ca*) has a beautiful offering: 12 renditions of the national anthem in Canada's most-spoken languages: in Punjabi, Tagalog, and Mandarin for starters. Via Rail offers in July, for 12-25 year-olds, a Summer Youth Pass for $150, anywhere in the country. And at UBC, an 800-year-old cedar log is being hand-carved into a reconciliation totem pole.

We look back, in order to look ahead with more resolve and better vision.

168

Two Faces of Peterborough
May 18, 2017

About three weeks ago, on two successive days, in two locations only blocks from one another, I saw two faces of Peterborough, radically different ones.

The first was with ten colleagues who volunteer with Amnesty International Group 46. I joined a discussion in the office of M.P. Maryam Monsef, Minister for the Status of Women.

We wanted to ask her about the $100 million new dollars just announced by the federal government in support of reducing gender-based violence.

Young Malala Yousafzai had just been in the House of Commons, becoming an honorary Canadian citizen. The nineteen-year-old from Pakistan had survived a gunshot wound to the head, and now is an advocate for the education of girls. Lest we be complacent, every night across Canada, 3500 women with their children are in shelters (in Peterborough, it's Crossroads), fleeing domestic violence.

The long-awaited inquiry into the 1200 missing and murdered Indigenous women and girls (MMIWG) has begun. The five appointed commissioners, I must add, are a most impressive group: four women and a man, all with Inuit and Indigenous roots.

Monsef told us that the national strategy to reduce gender-based violence would fund a "Centre of Excellence" to collect evidence on our national dilemma. She asked the Amnesty members for suggestions and mentioned the granting program run by Status of Women Canada. A local group might develop a project related to local needs and could be funded.

We went on to brief her about the damage done to Indigenous communities when workers from the extractive industries (read oil, gas and minerals) arrive in their numbers in a remote site, and either do not have a "social contract" to respect the residents, or do not abide by it.

Violence against women happens. Companies, we argued, bear the responsibility for the behaviour of their employees in such interventions.

Naturally, Amnesty International and a federal minister who is concerned about jobs and the economy, do not entirely see eye-to-eye on every issue and every emphasis. But it was an enlightening exchange of ideas and convictions. I walked home absorbed, and full of hope.

Contrast this day with the following one, which left me depleted, demoralized and indignant: my attendance in St Peter's Cathedral at the installation of the new Roman Catholic bishop of Peterborough.

A panorama of men, a procession of men, an altar full of men in tall white hats. In 2017! Sexist, unaware and patriarchal. Then the Knights of Columbus with swords and plumes.

This event had little to do with the quality of the persons involved. It was the system at show: the structures so unresponsive to modern thinking.

Right after my day discussing violence against women, I had to ponder what immediate good would be done for the world if the Roman church were to make a statement that men and women are equal, just that. And begin to model the value.

Conscious or unconscious, the exclusion of women that persists in my denomination speaks to the world with negative messages. Sometimes the world gasps: more often the young are perplexed and unlikely to commit to the institution as it looks today.

We feminists of faith hang on by our fingernails, convinced that patriarchy is in its last long throes. Humanity is damaged by it, religions disfigured and more pertinently, good is not done.

We also have a sense of humour, always useful for the long haul. On a Sunday recently dedicated to prayer for "vocations," we prayed for the ordination of women.

I saw a cheeky sign: "Ordain women or stop dressing like them!"

When the world's most numerous religion takes up the cause of gender justice, critiquing its own statements and practices and joining the movement, who knows the benefits that will flow.

For it and for all.

Salute to Doctors, or Adventures in the Medical System
June 1, 2017

You have seen those large newspaper ads asking us to salute our doctors by making a donation to PRHC? Well, I was moved to do so this week in gratitude to two, no actually, three, physicians who have tended me recently.

If you'd like to skip the health details, because there's nothing so boring as an old person reciting symptoms, stop reading here. But I will plunge on.

I was itching and tired. In what must have been quite a neighbourhood scene on Manning Avenue, I was out on the sidewalk one evening, lifting my shirt and showing my next-door neighbour, a young nurse, my skin.

"Ooohh" she said," that looks to me like shingles! I think you'd better go over to emergency right away and get a medication that needs to be taken within 72 hours, to lessen the severity."

"Emergency," I moaned. "That will be eight hours."

It was only three.

A kindly doctor apologized for making me wait, and then wrote out a prescription for an anti-viral. Ten minutes till Shoppers closes. There, a big sign greeted me at the desk: "Shingles can come after a chicken pox episode."

"Did you put this up for me?" I asked my pharmacist, Mike.

I began to feel better. Then I had pain, neuralgic pain that often comes with shingles. So I took myself to the After Hours Clinic and met another pleasant person. He gave me a mild something for pain. I read later that one of the remote side effects of this drug is suicidal thoughts. I know from American TV ads that dire side effects have to be mentioned to protect insurers. But my mood was improving. No watch needed here. I asked the doctor if there is a known cause of shingles. Should I cut back my activities?

He smiled and said, "I think you should just continue to go about spreading light and love." Since I was feeling grouchy, we had a good laugh at that. I think that doctor had a course in spiritual direction in college.

There's just a bit more.

I lived for six years in the tropics, and paid little attention to the sun. My nurse practitioner, Dee, noticed a suspicious lesion on my cheek. Off to a skin cancer surgeon. It was reassuring to know we have such a person in this town.

More adventure in the Medical Outpatients department at PRHC.

The doctor said, "Mrs Ganley, what kind of music do you like?"

Music? "Well," I stammered, "I like reggae, and classical."

"How about Yo Yo Ma playing a Bach fugue?" You bet. On it came through his small machine. He told me the ORs are often filled with music.

172

Then seriously, he asked me to tell readers that there is a lot of skin cancer in Peterborough. Outdoor and rural workers, now retired, who like me, paid little attention to old sol in their working days. He asked me to ask readers to take a close look at their skin and investigate anything suspicious. Two more skin specialists are coming here this summer.

I hope not to take up the time and attention of the medical system in the next year. I will work out at the Athletic Centre, and visit our seniors guru, Neli, in her fitness space in Lakefield. I will eat as the young people around here tell me: kale and tofu and all that stuff. I will take my blood pressure and get my eyes tested (incipient cataracts, they say).

But I am very thankful for the prompt, caring, even charming encounters I have had this spring. Here's to Drs Troughton, Heidman and Hamilton.

Wish it could be larger, but here goes a cheque to PRHC.

Fany and Ivin Come to Peterborough June 8, 2017

In the late seventies, around the time Jamaican Self-Help was starting up, another Peterborough family was having a similar inspiring experience in a poor southern country, and involving our community in supporting it: Jim and Anne McCallum.

The McCallums had volunteered in the impoverished central American country of Honduras, making connections with a remarkable nun, Sr Maria Rosa, who was rescuing abandoned and orphaned children from the mean streets of Tegucigalpa, the capital, and finding them homes in children's villages: secure, small communities where kids could live in small group homes led by an affectionate woman, a "tia" (auntie). They could finish high school, and afterwards attend a skill training centre in Tegucigalpa or in Santa Lucia.

Honduras, a country of 8 million people, has a very difficult history, with 50% of people living below the poverty line. Great damage was done by Hurricane Mitch in 1998, which killed 5000 people and destroyed 70% of the crops. In the United Nations Human Development Index, Honduras places 127 out of 188 countries.

In such conditions of deprivation, crime will thrive. In 2014, the American Peace Corps withdrew their volunteers, citing too much risk.

But dedicated people, both north and south, don't stop. The original group Horizons of Friendship, opened a fundraising thrift shop and office in Cobourg, and expanded to support projects in Nicaragua, Guatemala, El Salvador and Mexico.

The McCallums and supporters decided to maintain their steady involvement with Sr Maria Rosa and the children's villages in Honduras. Today, under president David Cain, the Friends of Honduran Children has an office in downtown Peterborough, and an employee, Allison, and raises thousands of dollars every year while sending scores of volunteers on service-learning trips to the village of Nuevo Paraiso in northern Honduras.

It has become clear that the education of girls is central to the development of individuals, families and communities. FoHC began to plan to sponsor two teenage Honduran girls from Nuevo Paraiso to come to Peterborough, live with a local family, learn English and enter Fleming College, with a goal of returning to their country to help their mother and siblings, and provide leadership for others.

Things took shape. Board member Dan Durst shepherded the project along. Fleming agreed to admit the girls, who are sisters, 19 and 17 years old, Fany and Ivin, under the Canadian, rather than the foreign rate. A Peterborough couple, Karen and Shannon Hartford, offered to provide a home and guidance for the sisters.

The Hartfords have been impressed by the resilience of the Honduran spirit, as they have watched the girls arrive in January cold, and adjust to an immensely different culture and lifestyle.

A month ago, having successfully completed their English-language proficiency test, Ivin and Fany gave a public talk at the Canoe Museum.

Through some tears, they told a powerful story of their determination, their loyalty to the mother who had to give them up to the children's village in 2009, and their gratitude for the opportunity to gain qualifications in business and computer science at Fleming. Fany and Ivin's mother had Ivin when she was 15, and now works as a maid in Tecucigalpa for C$25 a week.

It seems remarkable that the early eighties gave rise to at least three organizations in our region committed to overseas aid. Each attracted generous support.

What was it about the times? Was it that the leaders of the new initiatives were respected people rooted in their own work and communities, offering an opportunity for others to be globally-involved, to learn and be inspired? Was it the Canadian generosity towards others, even those beyond our borders?

Welcome, Fany and Ivin, and thank you for coming. You will learn, and so will we.

Solidarity with Filipina Women
June 15, 2017

In so many ways, we live in an amazingly good community. Let's look at just one Friday afternoon recently.

Four hundred people, mostly men of good will, tottered down George Street in red high heels, some of the shoes attached with duct tape to big male feet. These participants are aware of and stand (walk) against violence against women. They want to witness against it and to do good in the city.

That effort raised over $100,000 for Crossroads Shelter. Last year, I tried it too and it hurt, but it was so much fun and had such qualities of humour and hope.

Money is all-important for accomplishing good work. I know this fact well. The contraction of the services that Jamaican Self-Help could offer in the teeming ghettos of Kingston, Jamaica happened because our federal government at the time, 2012, cut matching funding.

But I also know that more than money is needed. Shelter provides service after the fact; after an abused woman and her kids have sought help. At least as relevant is the effort to prevent abuse, and to educate in healthy relationships. In the vein, a powerful kind of shared experience was offered that same day in this city.

At Peterborough Public Health on King Street, a meeting with an international focus and a deep poignancy took place. For two hours, a rich blend of local people, scholars and activists, Indigenous and non-Indigenous, mostly women, social workers and teachers, opened their minds and hearts to two health workers from the Philippines. Carin and Mark had come to show a gripping film about their work in the grim poverty of Manila, tell their stories, win friends and raise awareness.

The Philippines is in the grip of an autocratic president, Rodrigo Duterte, who has declared a war on drugs, and has stated he doesn't care who dies in the war. Mindanao is under martial law. People in the inner cities are afraid of drug informers and sometimes mistakenly distrust Likhaan.

How then, did this gathering happen here?

The estimable Julie Cosgrove, who for several years has led the Kawartha World Issues Centre, has long admired the work of Inter Pares, an Ottawa-based international development agency. Inter Pares approached Julie about their "Women's Health, Women's Rights" tour to ask if KWIC would partner in a Peterborough stop. Inter Pares was traveling with two people from its partner group in Manila, Likhaan, that works in women's health and sexual rights at the grassroots.

KWIC jumped at the chance to give Peterborough an opportunity to meet them, and rallied local partners.

Julie approached Dr Rosana Salvaterra, the respected Medical Officer of Health here, who once worked in India and has a global heart. The venue was secured.

The film shows Filipina women giving birth in distress, without trained attendants, and then being carried by neighbours on a chair to a hospital, hoping they will be admitted. It showed scenes of marital rape, and counselling in family planning. The resilience of the people and the community was palpable.

The visitors spoke being harassed by demonstrators outside their health clinics, people carrying signs emblazoned with "DEATH." Each initial stands, in English, for a sin it imagines Likhaan is promoting. "D" stands for divorce, "E" for euthanasia, "A" of course, for abortion, "T" stands for " Total Population Control" and "H" chastises homosexuality.

At the end of what must have been a harrowing presentation, one could feel the sympathy and understanding in the room. And a recognition that anti-woman attitudes are global.

Then who should come forward to take the visitors for food and relaxation in their own language but Carmela Valles, a Filipina-Canadian who was once head of the New Canadians Centre.

Thoughtful, profound and disturbing all at once.

Music Hath Charms
June 22, 2017

Is absolutely everyone in this city, maybe in this country, singing? For a weekend in May, it felt like that. And this summary doesn't even capture the night scene: coffee houses and pubs and jazz places and rooftops.

It covers just choral music: for large-group enthusiasts who have some training, an ability to carry a tune, a love of the voice, and the benefit of astute, charming directors.

I used to live in a culture where one heard singing daily on the streets and yards. Even on public transport. People moved about in a personal world they were creating, one of joy or often, of grief and lament, expressing it all with human voice and body rhythm and a lack of embarrassment.

Here in Canada, on the other hand, we value as much silence as we can get Or we listen to other voices singing on our many technical devices. It may seem that the art and pleasure of the spontaneous song are being lost.

But maybe, not so. The kids, the young ones, hum and chirp all around. And for the Peterborough concert-goer, it's been a gold mine.

The combined choirs of the Jubilaires for women and the Bonachords for men gave a rousing and patriotic public concert at Murray Street Baptist Church in May. The afternoon event was entitled *150, Eh?* and featured the gifted conductor Arlene Gray, who selected the songs and then commented wittily on the genesis of each.

True to the spirit of Canadiana, we heard *Lots of Fish in Bonavist Harbour*, and *Fare Thee Well, Love* from Newfoundland, *Song for the Mira* from Nova Scotia, and even the *Stoney Lake Song* sung by popular folksinger Bob Trennum. We crossed the country to include Ian Tyson's *Springtime in Alberta*, and the traditional *Red River Valley*.

There was acknowledgement of the Indigenous land, and a francophone song.

Nobody was having more fun than the 100 singers. Afterwards, Mike Peterman, who writes in these pages, said "I had to give up hockey but I took up singing!"

Of course, via Sudbury, Ontario came Stompin Tom's *The Hockey Song*. Words were displayed so we could all join in lustily.

178

Images of this vast and varied country were projected on large screens. Accompanying the two groups is an accomplished musician, Laurel Robinson-Lachance.

This was the very day after George Street United Church was filled to capacity to hear the Peterborough Singers, 100 more Peterburians of talent under the direction of Syd Birrell, offer several Mozart arias and a full rendition of the haunting *Requiem Mass*.

Music captures what we intuit but are often unable to express verbally: love of land, hope for the future, grief for loss, and gratitude for the environment. Even a happy birthday wish. These were all in the air in our community this spring.

So, riding high on popular and classical music, and as my personal "Canada 150" project, I took the plunge and bought a ticket to Toronto to the Canadian Opera Company's production of the opera *Louis Riel*.

A mighty new rendition of the fifty-year-old composition about the Metis rebel Louis Riel in 1880, a hero to many in western Canada, was staged by the COC and directed by John Hinton in the glorious glass building on Queen Street called the Four Seasons Centre for the Performing Arts.

The work was controversial from the beginning. Indigenous people found it unfair in its depiction of Riel as a villain. Hinton brought in fresher perspectives, with the addition of a kind of Greek chorus of Indigenous voices.

Riel was ultimately hanged by the colonial government for treason.

For an opera ingenue like me, it was good the words were projected in three languages above the stage: English, French and Cree.

I can't hum you a tune, but I learned a lot.

Pollinate or Perish
July 6, 2017

Warning: sexual content, as in insects.

I do wish I had paid more attention in high school to science, especially to botany. I was all too engrossed in the good-looking trigonometry teacher.

Now I have come to learn that pollination, which is responsible for two-thirds of our food supply, is at risk. That's because of climate change, loss of habitat and irresponsible use of pesticides (neonics).

Here are some terms for the discussion: "Pollination: the first step in the sexual reproduction process of plants. The transfer of a pollen grain from one flower's anthers to another flower's stigma."

And more: "The pollen grain contains 2 male sperm. They germinate the stigma, and a pollen tube grows. The sperm travel down the tube and one of them enters a female egg, which produces a seed." So there.

I did know that good things grow from seeds. I also knew that some forward-looking people in Norway have built a Global Seed Vault on an island called Svalbard, halfway between Norway and the North Pole. It hopes to protect our future and preserve seed diversity in any natural or man-made disaster. But let's not let it get that far.

Pollination makes the cereal crops grow, and the legume crops, and the fruits and vegetables. Pollination is achieved by animals, wind and water. The most excellent animals are the five "B's": beetles, bats, butterflies, bees and birds. So anything we can do to support these creatures is ultimately for our benefit.

"If you like to eat," says National Geographic, "thank the insects, particularly the bee."

So much I've been ignorant of. But when one of my friends, Jo Hayward-Haines of Ennismore, who is always ahead of the curve on issues, tells me we have a problem I listen.

The bad buzz, says Hayward-Haines, is that since 2006, there has been a huge decline in pollinating species. In 2010, the Rusty-patched bee was placed on the Ontario endangered species list. That makes action urgent.

Says pal Betty Borg, "I used to see swarms of bees around my apple tree. Now it's a good day if I see two bees."

In 2015, some concerned people formed a citizen's initiative called Peterborough Pollinators. Like almost everything I admire, it's volunteer. They educate. They plant. They lobby. They plan for 150 pollinator gardens in Peterborough this anniversary year. You can register yours or sign up to start one. The group meets monthly and has published an attractive 12-month calendar for 2017, chock full of facts and advice for every month of the year. (*www.peterboroughpollinators.com*) They collaborate with many groups and with the naturalists Drew Monkman and Jacob Rodenburg who wrote that marvelous *The Big Book of Nature Activities*.

I learned that the Kawarthas are home to 100 species of butterflies and 100 kinds of bees. I found out that monarch butterflies lay their eggs on milkweed after they have flown here from Mexico. I have seen pollinator gardens replace lawns: annuals such as sunflowers, cosmos, marigold, salvia and zinnias. Even the lowly dandelion has its uses in a healthy ecology.

The perennials include catnip, lavender, milkweed, bee balm, aster and sage. The virtuous veggies are tomatoes, peppers and eggplant. I now need a walkabout with an informed person. Three young women in town, Carlotta James, Megan Boyles and Kelly McDowell, are committed to building pollinator-friendly gardens through their social enterprise, Three Sisters Natural Landscapes.

It will take something of a cultural revolution for us to spurn the manicured lawn for the pollinator garden. But even I have become ill-at-ease at the sound of a power lawnmower. We may be on the threshold of realizing and respecting the inter-connections among all living things.

We can, as they say, be part of the solution.

Butterflies Ease Sorrow
July 20, 2017

This gig as a columnist (73 articles in three years so far) has me learning about Peterborough in many different ways. All of them have been relevant to my own living, and almost all have inspired me about the place where we live.

Today, the Bereaved Families of Ontario, Peterborough region. And it's personal.

Many years ago, a child of ours died of a sudden infection in Montreal. We were reeling in pain and shock. We had a two-year-old to comfort. We grieved in different ways and were for a while unable to help each other.

People rallied around us. My parents drove to Montreal from Northern Ontario, calm and accepting, even in their sorrow at the loss of their first grandchild. Our church community must have formed a roster of caregivers because we weren't alone for one evening for a full month. I took the pills put in front of me and drank the drinks.

Others planned a service that was both child-like and mature. The congregation wore white: the children from the nearby schools were there to both share and give hope. Awkward and caring teenagers came and shook hands.

There was no association to help us, but there were poems and readings, insightful books and articles - one especially, *The Bereaved Parent* by Harriet Schiff, which was a treasure.

So we carried on. The numbness eased. We went on a Marriage Encounter weekend. We had two more children.

Now today, fifty years on, kind and wise people have formed an association for bereaved families, here in our area. It has an office at Murray Street Baptist Church. It applied to the city in 2001, and got an utterly beautiful location at Millennium Park along the river, for its Butterfly Garden.

The BFO is a small, generous collective of basically four persons including Brian Ling, a psychotherapist in his working life, who says, "I cannot do other than this work," and Richard Jenkins, who grew up near Lindsay and with his wife Linda, tends the garden. He says, "It is simply the right thing to do."

Gary Beamish from Havelock tends to the paperwork: insurance and annual statements and so on. "I do this work to honour my fifteen-year-old son who died of leukemia."

He also serves on the board of the Ontario Bereaved Families Association. This coalition has 12 affiliate members across the province and organizes an annual conference. Peterborough serves a large area: Cobourg, Bancroft, Lindsay and points in between. The budget, from donations, is under $10,000 annually.

The genius, I think, is that each person who counsels is volunteer and has suffered the loss of a child. They are willing to spend time and talent comforting and reassuring newly bereaved family members, by phone or by email or in person.

Bereaved Families serves about 250 families a year here. There is a Christmas gathering, and a Butterfly Release Ceremony, when a new bronze plaque is ready to be installed. Jenkins gets the butterflies from a source in Lakefield. Wendy Rowan coordinates these gatherings. Right now, there are 11 plaques with 19 names each in the garden.

The BFO has noticed that while the need is ongoing, people today are not turning to traditional churches for consolation. There are many young single mothers who are grieving the death of a child but cannot afford a plot in a cemetery or a headstone.

The volunteers know how deeply appreciated is their work, and yet how invisible, even unknown, to many. Of Peterborough's many good works, I would rate Bereaved Families high on the list. I left our chat uplifted by the "kindness of strangers" to one another at the time of an experience that has been described as the worst occurrence one can suffer.

Phone 705 743 7233 Email: bfoptbo@gmail.com

Peterborough Judge in National Role
For August 3, 2017

I think it was rocker Bono of U2 fame, a thinking man and an Irish philanthropist, who first said that the world needs more Canada. Isn't that a nice compliment to our supposed virtues and attitudes? I've since heard M.P Maryam Monsef add that Canada also needs more Peterborough.

Every once in a while, I hear about some Peterburian making a real, often quiet, national contribution to our country.

Meet Ontario Superior Court Justice Barry MacDougall of Walkerfield Avenue.

In this year of our 150th anniversary, there is renewed attention in the mainstream culture, along with some shame and a strong desire to make things right with Indigenous people. MacDougall has taken on an assignment, one of five justices from across the country to do so, to try to bring to a settlement claims by native bands for redress of an historic wrong done to them by the Crown (Canadian government).

It is the Specific Claims Tribunal, set up by Minister of Indian Affairs Jim Prentice in 2008. The going has been slow. Our country has 1.8 million First Nations, Inuit and Metis people, representing almost 6.5% of the population.

There are 600 bands, some with as few as 250 members, others with 4500 and more. Half of Indigenous people live off-reserve. And there are 863 reserves. Before the release of the Royal Commission Report on Indigenous People in 1996, the complaints from any band council about land, or the handling of money due to them were dealt with by civil servants who decided the merits of the claim.

One strong recommendation was that an independent body be set up to adjudicate such claims. The government of Canada agreed to establish a Specific Claims Tribunal, made up of Superior Court judges.

The purpose was to give bands an opportunity to be heard instead of going to court, a process which can be costly, lengthy and at times adversarial and unsatisfactory. MacDougall, born in Timmins and educated at the University of Toronto, came to Peterborough in 1969, and practiced law until being appointed to the Superior Court of Ontario in 1995.

A wide reader and student of culture, whom I once saw reading Alice Munro's *The Progress of Love* at the Trent bookstore, MacDougall has an affable personality and a desire to contribute to Canada. He met Judge Murray Sinclair of the recent Truth and Reconciliation Commission two years ago.

The mandate of the Tribunal is to discern the validity of the claim, and then decide on the compensation to be paid. He or she is not allowed to return land itself. Ideally, the hearings are just a few days in length. The judge goes to the reserve, in civilian clothes, not judicial robes, and sits in the Community Hall. The meetings are open to the public.

Generally, MacDougall says, Indigenous women are leading this work.

There are hundreds of claims waiting in the wings to be heard. He has been shocked by the data revealed: up until the sixties, native people had to have permission to leave the reserve.

"We have a dark side to our history to be reckoned with," he says. "Stereotypes are still present and much education is needed for Canadians in general. We need to realize we have been patronizing and discriminatory."

"A judge today hearing these grievances is now somewhat shielded from the emotional impact of the wrongs because the cases are historical. But the experience has been profound for me, and very enlightening as I come to my 75th year."

"I have just come back from taking a course in Boston at the Harvard School of Mediation. There were participants from around the world. The idea of mediation as a replacement for litigation in many cases is gaining ground. I hope I can contribute to this movement in the law."

Difficult but Necessary Planning
August 17, 2017

There's something about reaching four-score years that tends to focus the mind.

Grateful for so much living, for great joy in my relationships, and for pride in my country's achievements, I am getting my affairs, as they say, in order. Insofar, of course, that such a thing is possible in an uncertain world. My sister tells me I am realistic to a fault. But I am convinced our culture hurts itself by so thoroughly denying death and all discussion of it.

So I'll start.

I often consult the website *Dying with Dignity,* which is always up-to-the-minute with information and advocacy. We now have "MAID" in Canada, Medical Assistance in Dying, and it is a changing the scene for sure. Some 69% of doctors decline in conscience to participate in MAID, and they have every right to do so. The remaining number suffices for the need, which is essentially small, about one percent of deaths. There were 385 instances of MAID in Ontario last year, and about 100,000 deaths.

This enabling national legislation is a work in progress, and needs ongoing study. Are the safeguards robust enough? Should the conditions be widened (i.e. to include advance instruction for profound dementia)?

MAID is now the law, and publicly-funded hospitals, even religious ones, do not have the right, as some Catholic hospitals have done (St. Paul's, Vancouver, for one), to refuse patients or turn them out when they seek MAID if all other conditions have been met: assessments by two physicians, generous time to decide, the ability to change one's mind and the presence of an severe illness that will bring death within a foreseeable future.

I noticed that the City of Peterborough is encouraging those laggards among us to make a will, as seen in a street-wide banner downtown.

I also copied a 4-page *Advance Care Directive* from the *Dying with Dignity* site, and filled it out. It has no force in law and it needs no witnesses, but it clarifies some choices at life's end, and serves as guidance for loved ones in dire situations. It can prevent family conflict, all too common. Just ask lawyers and doctors about family fights on "what mother would want." Let mother spell it out beforehand. Some of the treatments you can express your wishes about, include the use of antibiotics, ventilation and blood transfusions. And organ donation.

Then there is the DNR, the "Do Not Resuscitate" form. Believing that these things are best done when one is well and optimistic, I went to see my doctor. The form is now available only from a health professional. Paramedics absolutely need to see it in emergency situations when one has collapsed and is unconscious. Without directions to the contrary, they will resuscitate.

My DNR is in the freezer section of the fridge.

While there is evidence that our cultural avoidance of this topic is lessening, there is a long way to go. Some book clubs have been discussing Dr Atul Gawande's excellent book, *Being Mortal.* Hospice Peterborough can hardly keep a copy in stock for borrowing.

Feeling utter dread at the completion of life has a disabling effect. The religions can help, but many western minds, not drawn to scripture, have poetry. We are spiritual beings. Emily Dickinson wrote: "I believe we shall in some manner be cherished by our Maker." Rumi, the Muslim mystic, wrote, "The One who had led you so far will lead you further." Poet Yeats of Ireland said, "I will arise and go now and go to Innisfree."

Raymond Carver asked, "And did you get what you wanted in this life, even so?/ I did/ What did you want?/ To call myself beloved, to feel myself beloved of the earth."

Death discussions while difficult, can be deeply satisfying.

TandemEyes ~ Going for a Ride
August 24, 2017

Never underestimate the power of Peterborough women meeting at a local gym in 2011 to see a need and set about meeting it.

Anne Wood and Brenda Tindale, together with three other women, hatched a creative plan to start a club in Peterborough called TandemEyes. This cycling club enables people with vision loss to enjoy cycling on a tandem bike paired with a sighted volunteer. The group rides Monday and Wednesday evenings each week in the months May through August for two hours. They begin and end their rides at Silver Bean Café in Millennium Park. The cyclists ride in a group in what has become a dynamic sight in the community.

The community involvement in TandemEyes has been strong, and has grown over the past five years. Several people, who prefer to remain anonymous, has donated four tandem cycles, each worth $3000. Princess Gardens Retirement Home which is nearby, stores the tandems. Many local businesses have supported TandemEyes, including Wild Rock Outfitters, Fontaine's Sports and Cycle, and the BIKE Community Shop. Active Together, a project of the Council for Persons with Disabilities and the Ontario Visually Impaired Golfers Association (OVIG), have each donated a tandem.

Each year, TandemEyes has applied for and received funds from the City of Peterborough Community Grants, which helps with bike maintenance. The Peterborough Cycling Club has sponsored Tandem Eyes since the beginning. It provides financial support and has donated a tandem.

"This is an unique arrangement," says Wood. "We are integrated into a mainstream community bike club, not set aside as a separate program. Erasing stigma is what we are about."

The two women developed a website for additional information. "Most riders come by way of word-of-mouth," says Tindale. "We would like people interested in volunteering to hear about us. Volunteers are the most important part of the club since everything we do is based on the generosity of others."

"We always need captains," says Wood. "Many people with vision impairment are socially isolated and physically inactive. We hope to change this. We are integrated age and gender-wise."

There is a broad range of backgrounds among the captain: teachers, retirees, students. Many have been with the program since its beginning. About 32 people are actively involved.

"Communication is all important," says Wood. The captains provide details about the ride, the landscape, the river, the plant growth and paths, as the ride goes along. "It is a partnership of trust," she adds.

Safety is a main priority. Every spring, training sessions are given to both "captains," the sighted riders, and to "stokers," the people who are visually impaired. The bikes themselves are seven feet long, and manoeuvring them takes some balance and lots of communication. All stokers wear a bright best for easier visibility.

Peter Laurie, who teaches at Fleming College, tells me TandemEyes is a highlight of his summer: real, practical, outdoors and active.

"There is a great sense of freedom and an experience of the outdoors and of movement so often difficult for the vision-impaired," says Tindale. "I want to give something back to this good community I live in."

The women find it hard to estimate the number of hours they give to the set-up, the pairings, contacting and grant writing. Rainy weather this year has made this all more time-intensive.

One concern they have is with the transportation needs of the stokers to get to and from the ride centres.

TandemEyes is a down-to-earth activity, which depends on the generosity of citizens. It is useful and educational, pleasurable and helpful, low in cost and high in volunteer spirit, all aspects of a healthy community.

Watch for it Mondays and Wednesdays after 6 pm until the end of August, and give a cheer. *www.tandemeyes.com*

Walking for Wisdom: The Camino in Spain September 7, 2017

When I first told friends that I intended to walk some of the pilgrimage route across northern Spain, the Camino de Santiago, I got lots of tips and suggestions.

In fact, there are a number of Peterburians who have taken on this project: Fred and Karen Kooy (more than once), Kate Jarrett and Sheila Collett, Betsy McGregor, Michael Gibson, Barb Woolner, Julie Fitzpatrick, Bev Robson, Eloise Bucholtz and many more. We must have a get-together later this fall to share stories.

Two bits of advice I have hung on to were these: "Make every step a prayer." That perhaps won't be too hard: I am generally a praying person. My longest day will be 18 kilometers, and shortest 11. That makes quite a few steps.

The other was: "Put on a medieval mind." Now that could be a challenge. I am a post-modern, somewhat technocratic, educated, skeptical, feminist writer. My culture has been through the Reformation and the Enlightenment and the age of science. This is no longer the Age of Faith. I live in an interconnected global world which has managed to produce 7 billion people, and to create massive threats to itself by its profligate consumption and war-mongering.

Medieval Europe on the other hand, had only 65 million persons, almost every one a Christian Catholic. Most were peasant, and they believed in God, in the Christian gospel, and in the Pope and the King. Most were very poor. One-third of the population undertook the pilgrimage. A few were prisoners serving their sentence this way!

All had a deep sense of their own sinfulness and need for forgiveness. Pilgrimages, whether to Rome or Jerusalem, which were the most popular routes, or to Santiago de Compostela, the third most popular, were acts of devotion and healing - people making acts of contrition so that punishment for sins would be removed.

Some of these concepts of spirituality, which we have moved away from, could now be at least partly re-appropriated, if I am to get out of this walk all it promises. It is amazing to realize that the pilgrimage to this north-western Spanish city has been going on since the ninth century, over 1000 years. I'll be in the footsteps of St. Francis of Assisi (he actually took a donkey), royals Ferdinand and Isabella, and the present King of Spain.

In the 11th and 12th centuries, the walk was dangerous, with brigands and robbers. So the Pope introduced a set of knights, the Knights Templar, to protect the pilgrims. Eventually, the knights, who were a kind of bank, became too powerful and were eliminated by kings and popes. Rough times.

Under my feet will be roads built first by the Romans before the Common Era, when they invaded Spain (then called Hispania).

When Martin Luther launched his reformation of the Catholic church 500 years ago this fall in Germany, piety of this kind fell out of favour. It wasn't until the 1980's that interest began to take hold again. In 1986, 20,000 pilgrims came to the Camino: in 2016, 200,000 did. (Only 56 were over 80 years of age. 60 used wheelchairs. And there were 143 nationalities.)

The Spanish government has introduced a series of pilgrim hostels: basic dormitory accommodation, no reservations - just show up. Much of this part of Spain is rural and poor. So peregrinos are welcome as an economic boon.

I expect to meet all kinds of people walking for all kinds of reasons: to quit smoking, to lose weight, to get over a relationship, to enjoy the outdoors. This Spain will include steep mountains and a vast dry desert (la meseta). It will include many villages and a few cities of note. For a good picture of the landscape, see Martin Sheen's feature film, *The Way*.

Next article; the destination, the cathedral-city of Santiago, and some preparation.

The Camino and the Lakefield Connection September 14, 2017

In 1985, I was teaching literature at Lakefield College School. A tall young man, age 16, arrived as a new student. He was from Spain: Prince Felipe, heir to the throne occupied by his father, King Juan Carlos, and his mother, Queen Sophia.

A mild, shy lad, he fit in unobtrusively for his year of study, and enjoyed cross country running all along the concession roads of Douro-Dummer.

One feature that amazed us was that he came with three security guards from Spain. It was a time in Spanish politics of a violent independence movement in the northern Basque country. There had been attacks and deaths. (Spain and its Basque population came to a peace agreement in 2011.)

Head Terry Guest of Lakefield had experience with royalty coming to the school, having had Prince Andrew of the UK in 1977. Seeking to keep the school normal, he asked that the Spanish security people live in the village, not on campus. This worked well for the year. I think they were pretty bored.

192

I recall the graciousness of the Queen at the graduation dance, gamely dancing with all the teenage boys, never mind the threat to her feet.

Spanish recent history is astounding. For thirty years after the Spanish Civil war (1936-39), a dictator, Generalissimo Francisco Franco ruled Spain, supported by Hitler and Mussolini. Before he died in 1975, he decreed that he be succeeded by King Juan Carlos. Surprise! The king ushered in a transition to democracy and a constitutional monarchy. His son, a young man Felipe has become King Felipe VI of Spain, now married to a former TV host, Queen Letizia, with a family of two daughters. He sailed for his country at the Olympics. He returned 20% of his salary when Spain was undergoing economic hardship. I just saw him on TV visiting survivors of the Barcelona attack.

Now 32 years later, I am going to Spain to the main city of Basque country, Bilbao, and starting my pilgrimage to the cathedral city of Santiago. The whole distance is 700 kilometres, but my ambition is just 156 kilometres. Did I say "just"?

St Augustine in 400, said, "All things are solved by walking." I realize I am much too car-dependent. So my training has included walks, with a stick and my good hiking shoes, all over town.

I visited my physiotherapist, Connor. He adjusted my backpack. I was wearing it too low. He did the same with my collapsible walking pole, gave me four morning stretch exercises and advised me to get a hydration backpack. Now that's something pokey: the sucking and the accessing water.

I read 11 books on the Camino, from the truly pious (Sr Joyce Rupp's *Walk in a Relaxed Manner*) to the hilarious (Tim Moore's *Spanish Steps* about dragging a donkey across the route: donkeys don't take to bridges), to the ridiculous Shirley MacLaine. And a novel by David Lodge called *Therapy*.

193

Perhaps best of all, I found a roommate, Arapera, who is a 73 year-old Maori widow from New Zealand. Her tribe is the Ngati Kahungunu (61,000 members). I expect to learn a lot from her.

What is in some doubt is the "holiness" of my pilgrimage. Our bags are transported to the next place of rest, leaving us with just a day pack. Our night bookings are made by the organizer. I am past the point of "winging" it, not knowing where I sleep, or arriving at a hostel and finding it full.

A friend sent me some notes about undertaking a pilgrimage. "Traveling," said writer Bruce Chatwin, "is not merely a spiritual act, it is the self's purest expression. It is a sloughing-off of the world." Not conventionally religious, Chatwin nonetheless wrote, "My God is the God of Walkers."

I'm giving it a try this month.

Moments of Transcendence
September 21, 2017

In 2004, an accomplished Toronto musician, Oliver Schroer, with his wife and two friends, walked the Camino. He was ill with cancer, only 48, and he said, "In my backpack, my violin like a wooden chalice, like my own precious relic, and a portable recording studio."

As he walked, over 1000 kilometres, he entered chapels and churches, sat down, played original music and recorded. It was, he said, "Music called forth by the landscape and the pain in my feet."

Many places had appealing acoustics. "New pieces came, one hill, one valley at a time." Once he was chased from a church by a sacristan crying, "You have to have permission of the bishop!"

Schroer died in 2008, at the age of 52. I listened to this music as I read books and prepared for my walk. The story of how this northwestern Spanish city came to be famous as the goal of long pilgrimages starting from all over Europe, is shrouded in time, legend and a shred of forensic evidence.

It is said that James, the brother of John, both sons of Zebedee, those men called "son of thunder" by Jesus because of their fiery natures, were dispatched after the crucifixion to far off lands to preach. James landed in Spain where he attracted only a few followers. He headed back to Jerusalem, and was beheaded in 44 AD by Herod Agrippa.

The plot thickens. It is said his followers took his bones back to Spain by sea, landed on the Atlantic coast and buried the bones. Their boat acquired cockleshells on its hull. These scallop shells have become the symbol of the Camino, today, seen everywhere marking the route.

No further mention is made of James for 750 years. Then, a monk said he was led to a field of stars, and did some digging. There were remains of three persons. The site began to be regarded as sacred. In 852, St. James is said to have appeared to the Spanish as they were resisting the Moors who had invaded from Morocco in 712. The Moors conquered Hispania and ruled, leniently, for 700 years, building grand architecture, the best of which is the Alhambra in Granada.

I won't be seeing this grandeur, but before even starting my walk, I was able to spend some time in the magnificent Guggenheim Art Museum in Bilbao. It took me a while to figure out the "Guggenheim" connection, since New York City has a spiral masterpiece designed by the late Frank Lloyd Wright and named "the Guggenheim." Samuel Guggenheim, it turns out, was a wealthy American arts patron. His foundation sponsored this Spanish museum, which opened in 1997 along the river Nervion, a titanium, glass and concrete marvel designed by Canadian-American Frank Gehry.

I was one of a million visitors this year.

The museum in Bilbao has lifted this industrial city on the Bay of Biscay, a city of 300,000, to new heights. A cultural installation can do that.

Then, one cannot fail to be moved by the phenomenon of the botafumiero, a huge incense-burner in the Santiago Cathedral at the Pilgrims' Mass at the end. It emits incense as it burns charcoal, flying up to the ceiling in a 90-foot arc set in motion by eight strong men wearing red robes and pulling 3-inch ropes. It hesitates at the top of the cathedral and then comes roaring down, skimming the heads of worshippers. The censer is 80 kilos in weight and almost two metres in height. It travels at 68 kph. Enough to open heaven, I guess.

These make memories enough to meditate on for a long time. I was a kind of pilgro-tourist seeking, and sometimes finding. All hail to Espana (and its wine).

The NDP Leadership
October 5, 2017

On Sunday October 1, first ballot results catapulted Ontario MP Jagmeet Singh into the leadership of the New Democratic Party. The first person of colour to lead a Canadian political party, Singh was an early favorite in the mail-in four person race.

Some of my NDP friends had voted for Niki Ashton, some for Charlie Angus.

Having looked at the party site, and read about the four candidates, I sent a little donation to candidate Niki Ashton. Among the four candidates who sought the leadership to replace former leader Thomas Mulcair, another worthy person was Charlie Angus, whom I have known from Northern Ontario, and from editing his popular columns for the newspaper Catholic New Times in Toronto from 2001-2006.

I sent a donation to Charlie's campaign, too.

196

Primarily I donate, small but real, because I am a participating citizen. I was touched by a remark of an American Hispanic woman a while ago: "I don't want to be a star, just a member of the constellation." Only 3% of Canadians belong to a political party of any kind. That to me is a shame. I've never believed that voting every few years is enough.

I participate also because I believe we are a much better country because of the third party. It historically has developed policies from labour and the "left," keeping in focus working people and the marginalized. The NDP has influenced the centre, and even at times the right-wing of the political spectrum, and has formed public opinion very successfully. Even sometimes it has formed government, never federally, but often provincially.

Its very presence, intellectual energy and appeal to conscience have been copied by other parties. Think Medicare, labour law, environmental awareness, poverty. For another thing, it prevents us from sliding into the hostile situation that now prevails in our southern neighbour: two parties; acrimonious, "take no prisoners" attitudes, open racism, and the ascent to power of a totally unsuitable leader.

The NDP chose not to have a convention for this contest, but to have its registered members vote online or by mail between Oct 1-15. Each candidate needed to have 500 signatures from across the country and from several demographic groups, and then to have a $30,000 entry fee. The ballot was a preferential, ranked one.

Though not a party member, I was favouring Niki Ashton , a 35 year-old and MP from Churchill, Manitoba since 2008. She speaks Greek as well as French and English, her mother being a feminist activist of Greek origin - her father an NDP provincial member.

Ashton's policies included confronting growing inequality in Canada. The stats about increasing wealth and increasing poverty bear this necessity out.

197

She has challenged the incarceration system that seems to target Indigenous people, calls for universal child care, and a medical plan that includes pharmacare, dental care and services for mental health. Her goal is a carbon-free economy. She speaks for tuition-free post-secondary education.

It is probable that her stance on the Israel-Palestine conflict that is bravest. She has been almost a lone voice in Parliament calling for Palestinian solidarity in this painful and long-standing situation. It is not a popular cause in Canada, and the pro-Israel lobby is strong.

The Montreal-based NGO, "Canadians for Peace and Justice in the Middle East" gave her a star rating. She has long criticized the Israeli government for building settlements on Palestinian lands, and for human rights abuses in the conflict. Ashton calls for justice for Palestinians and a solution that tackles the underlying roots of the conflict. She opposes Canadian arms sales of all kinds to the Middle East. She supports the anti-Israeli-government campaign called "BDS: Boycott, Divest and Sanction."

The fact that Niki Ashton is at the moment pregnant with twins didn't hurt her cause with me. Let's hope she has influence in her party going forward.

The Camino Walk: What Did I Learn?
October 12, 2017

I have a deepened interest in history. Think of Spain: today it is a constitutional monarchy, a country of 46 million people with some sharp regional stresses, a member of the European Union, and the producer of scores of artists and writers. In Spain, over time, rule has been by the Romans, the Christians, the Muslims, the Christians again, the Fascists, and now secular, democratic humanists.

I learned something of my limits. 18 km is absolutely the farthest any human should walk in a day. Earplugs have not yet been created that work for me.

Sometimes you have to act before you know the meaning of your actions. Robert Sibley of *The Ottawa Citizen* who walked with his son, advises that one adopt the traditional practices of pilgrimage regardless of one's religious skepticism. Forego, he says, all the diversions of our consumer society that keep us from thinking too much.

I learned about the friendship of strangers, the wildness of the divine, the slowing down of life to a pedestrian pace. One of my companions, age 73, fell and cut her forehead. Immediately two Irish nurses, walking along behind, had their kits out. Absolutely everyone, overtaking you or not, bids you "Buen Camino." There was what we called the "hippie compound," where a barefoot fellow offered fresh fruit, and three passing Mexicans sang in harmony in an impromptu concert.

I learned that New Age mysticism offers answers that don't satisfy me. Yet mindless materialism is worse.

Faith and doubt co-exist. Walking is still the most popular way to go: there's also cycling, and donkey-leading. There are 100 different routes from all over Europe. All are heading west, all with the sun at their backs.

It was not so much transformation as consolidation for me. All those miles of silence to think, while moving one's body and not knowing what the rest of the day would hold. Some convictions became clearer for my life. Make poetry a priority: Tennyson, Levertov, Mary Oliver, T.S. Eliot, Margaret Atwood, Raymond Carver and so on.

Simplify and declutter even more. Can I go car-less? Eliminate red meat? Even eliminate flying? Continue to support centre-left politics. I choose that position for strategic reasons, but my personal positioning is left. Maintain a feminist vision. So much has been accomplished for female equality in these last 50 years, and so much is left to do to make it global.

199

Nurture gratitude, as Canadian society goes about defining itself and acts in relation to our troubled southern neighbour. Theologian Richard Niebuhr said: "Pilgrims are persons in motion, passing through territories not their own, seeking something we might call completion." Added the Talmud, "When a man's passions bewilder him, he should put on black clothes and travel to a place where he is not known."

About two-thirds of the way along the Camino route there is a giant iron cross high about the ground, surrounded by millions of small stones: pilgrims have left their burdens, their hopes, their grief. It is called the Cruz de Ferro.

I had asked some family and friends if they wanted to give me a small stone. So in my bag I had two little crystals from sick friends, a tiny bag of earth from our old home on Aberdeen Avenue, a lovely rock from the North Saskatchewan River collected by an Edmonton grandson, a dragonfly bookmark shaped out of wire from BC, a lock of hair from a 12-year-old granddaughter, and John's nametag from our CIDA briefing in Ottawa in 1975.

At the Cruz de Ferro, I laid these all out, in deep thought, while my Aussie companions took pictures. Done and done. Except that Barb Woolner and I are hosting a one-time Camino reunion at Sadleir House for anyone interested, on October 26 at 5.30 pm.

Violence Against Women Persists
October 19, 2017

Almost sixty years ago, at the beginning of "Phase Two" of the women's movement for equality, a wise American writer, Rosemary Radford Ruether said, "This massive global movement for equality is similar in scope to the Industrial Revolution. It will take 200 years."

What then are we to make of 2017?

I personally have lived among consciousness-raised and equality-practising men all my life: my family, my neighbours, my co-workers, employers, the people I read and consult. There is now enormous well-being for women of a certain age, race and social class.

I have felt safe everywhere I have lived; in 3 countries and several cities. Only one episode of invasion of my space happened, when I was 12 years old, and the trusted family handyman did some groping. I was too confused and embarrassed to tell anyone.

But social analysis and statistics tell another story. Worsened by our toxic celebrity culture and the nastiness on the internet, male entitlement over women continues to loom large. A U.S. president boasts of his sexual mastery, 3700 Canadian women with their 2000 children seek shelter across the country each night.

School girls everywhere are harassed. The world religions are hardly any help. Globally, 750 million girls are married off before they are 18 years old. Half of all Canadian women report they have been assaulted, verbally or physically.

Culture is not changing fast enough. Although framed as a women's issue, it really is a men's problem and must be confronted by all. Certainly education of both genders is crucial. All the young parents I know are doing it. Locker rooms are going to change.

My daughter-in-law, with two sensitive-to-the-news girls, tells them: "In a sad or bad situation, always look for the helpers." That's a bit of wisdom I try to incorporate.

So I spoke with the Kawartha Sexual Assault Centre's Executive Director Sonya Vellenga. KSAC marked 40 years in Peterborough with a gala at Sadleir House on October 14, at which one of the volunteer founders, Sara Fernald came from Atlanta, Georgia, to speak of the early days.

She reflected on the fact that while there was disbelief, there were also many who stood by to help, including men.

One of the signature programs of KSAC is entitled *MENding: Engaging Men to End Gender Violence*. It also has an innovative project with the 19 teams of the Ontario Hockey League. Locally, the Petes advise young athletes and model respectful behaviours towards girls and women.

"The Mane Intent" is an initiative that enables girls who have experienced trauma to build self-esteem through work with animals at a nearby horse farm. A meditative walking program draws over 15 women with the same healing goals.

At KSAC's office on Water Street, 3 full-time employees counsel about 150 women each year. Three more work on community education and crisis support. The budget is modest: $483,000 annually, including funds from the Ontario Ministry of the Attorney General, Status of Women Canada and the United Way of Peterborough. Other donations from private fundraisers and Delta Bingo are received.

In 2015, an important 48-page report authored by Lisa Clarke of KSAC was published. *Lessons from Behind the Door* looked at Peterborough responses to violence against women, including that against Indigenous and LGBTQ women.

There are 14 agencies in our region providing various services to victims and education programs for the community. Patriarchy is an old and stubborn foe.

These agencies include the public school board, the Police Department, the YWCA, Peterborough Youth Services, Public Health, the City Social Services, the Elizabeth Fry Victim Services and the college and university.

Gregory Baum: Happy Warrior in Religion
October 26, 2017

I've always been intrigued by theology. While acknowledging the sharp critique of it as "the study of nothing," I nonetheless pursued the study of theology as an academic discipline at the post-secondary level and beyond.

There were a few reasons for this. One, to be sure, was personal. Faced with those darn questions, "Who am I?" "Where is here?" and "Who are all those other people?" throughout our lives, I wanted to have a look at what other minds have thought and said. Closely associated with those three questions is the one: "How shall I live?"

The second reason was that I enjoyed it. The stretching of the mind. Sometimes inspired, sometimes shocked and appalled, sometimes even amused, but always engaged. Ultimately, I thought it a useful and provocative study.

In the Middle Ages, theology was considered "the queen of the sciences." It was respectable, even necessary, to study theology, and of course in the West, that was Christian theology. Then, it was largely abandoned in universities as obscurantist, its claims too hard to prove.

Today, theology is making a modest comeback, especially comparative religious studies. I think the faster universities set up departments of religious studies, and hire broad-minded scholars, who may or may not adhere to one or other tradition, the better.

The third reason was theology's influence, sometimes subtle, sometimes overt, on the fate of the world and the politics of culture. As a dawning feminist, I soon saw the negative effects of most religions on the status of real women. It hasn't been entire or wholesale of course: Catholicism has had the heroic Virgin Mary; Hinduism, the smart Saraswati; Islam, the leadership of Khadijah; and the Jews, the wisdom of Sarah and Miriam.

Still, patriarchs have uniformly used divine figures to control and suppress women.

With excitement, then, I've read scores of works by feminist thinkers working within the faiths, not outside them. Pakistan-born Riffat Hassan of the University of Kentucky proclaimed, "There are 600 million Muslim women in the world: most are poor and illiterate. I cannot reach them through the Universal Declaration of Human Rights: I can reach them through the Koran."

The moral leaders of our world: M.L. King, the Dalai Lama, Mother Teresa, Gandhi, Nelson Mandela all claim a religious tradition. We need to be always on the alert for false claimants too, as American politics so well illustrates.

Which brings me long way around to my sadness at the death of the great humanist-theologian Gregory Baum, Canadian, age 94, in Montreal this week.

A cheery theologian, who in one lifetime had been all of these: a Jewish refugee from Belin at age 17, a Roman Catholic monk from 1947 to 1974, a hugely important theologian, a key ally of Pope John XXIII who almost singlehandedly improved relations between his Church and the other religions, especially the Jewish community; a married man who wrote 20 books and taught theology and ethics at both the University of Toronto and McGill University, and finally a self- disclosed gay man (*The Oil Has Not Run Dry*, 2017).

A Montrealer said this week, "He was a brilliant, buffeted and loving theologian." Baum founded the influential magazine *The Ecumenist*, and edited it from 1962 to 2004. He championed the rights of Catholics to birth control, and the ordination of women, bearing the condemnation of some in his church with courage. He constantly reminded the Church that it changes. "I do think there is a kind of pluralism in life," he said, and greeted the election of Pope Francis with delight.

A Quaker friend of mine wrote this week: "I heard Gregory Baum at Waterloo in the 1970's. He deeply affected my thinking. He said the Trinity could be understood as three C's: community, critique and call."

Gregory Baum, my kind of theologian, RIP.

"We Vote CBC - Peterborough" Speaks Out
November 2, 2017

The Globe and Mail had a recent article asserting that Canadian discussion at every level of society is much more civil than that which exists in the U.S.

Many observers agree, and put a lot of credit for that on the public institutions fostered here, especially in the media, such as the arms-length, publicly-funded Canadian Broadcasting Corporation. In fact, Peterborough has had an active and influential watchdog group for several years, lobbying for sustained funding and better leadership for the CBC.

On the question of governance, it remains true that of the nine directors of the CBC, seven are donors to the Conservative Party, including the Chair, Remi Racine and the president, Hubert Lacroix.

To its credit, the new government has put in place a process for choosing directors, setting up a credible advisory committee including actor Colm Feore, Indigenous film-maker Alanis Obamsawin, and broadcaster Tom Clarke to advise on new appointments to the board, as vacancies occur this year and next. Such people are to be "non-partisan, qualified and representative."

The local group called "We Vote CBC-Peterborough," a committee of eight persons including Kady Denton, Roy Brady, Al Buchkowski, Richard Lowery, John Anderson, Peter Currier and Susan Hubay, is now responding to Minister Melanie Joly's speech of September 28. It had been two years in the making, since the Liberals won the federal election of 2015.

It was a 28-page framework for culture policy, called *Creative Canada: a Vision for Canada's Creative Industries.*

Mme Joly called for "investing in our creators and their stories, promoting Canadian content at home and abroad, strengthening public broadcasting and supporting local news."

"Friends of Canadian Broadcasting," a national, independent group, has given it a C-rating. "We Vote CBC-Peterborough" agrees. They criticize the paper for many weaknesses.

"The Minister" they say, "has left unaddressed the local media crisis and the urgent problem of how to staunch the flow of Internet advertising dollars to foreign media companies, giants such as Netflix and Google. We must assert Canadian sovereignty over the Internet, just as the government did at the dawn of the TV age. Money is flowing south, money needed for Canadian media, as fast as snowbirds to Florida in March. American giants enjoy significant and unfair advantage over Canadian competitors. These companies operating in Canada should pay sales tax, such as the HST."

On the real possibility of local news outlets being shuttered, the group calls for the money saved from closing tax loopholes to be used to support local news to ensure survival in small and medium markets.

Scant mention is made of print journalism, which is a shame. Joly's paper was focussed on public broadcasting, which is where Canadians will turn as newspapers fold. One in three journalist jobs have disappeared since 2010. Take a look at the hard-working *Examiner* newsroom: five excellent journalists where once there were 16. Guelph has lost its daily paper. I cannot think that "the digital revolution" can in any way compensate for this.

These Peterborough citizens of "We Vote CBC" care deeply about citizenship, and the role that public broadcasting plays in giving all of us a sense of perspective and responsibility. The CBC has a mandate to "inform, enlighten and entertain" our news and our stories, not the message of a corporation or a political party.

They keep in touch with MP Maryam Monsef and actively lobby with well-informed argument. They can mobilize some 3000 citizens in our area. Concerned about the sale of CBC buildings and the slow action on new board appointments, "We Vote CBC' continues its work. They contribute to the ongoing conversations started by Minister Joly.

Aware that the CBC must expand digital services, they nonetheless retain a special fondness for radio!

Their voice of reason is badly needed going forward as this "vision" announced by Minister Joly takes shape.

Acts of Human Goodness: East and West November 16, 2017

I'm just home from Edmonton, (minus 14 degrees), where I had gone to check in on three teenage grandchildren, ages 13, 15 and 17. They are thriving in their downtown high school, where Alberta premier Rachel Notley's kid goes.

All are entirely bilingual, one rides a horse. She has actually met the cast of CBC's *Heartland*, oh joy. The grandson plays Mozart on the piano, but declines to earn certificates or credits for that pleasure. The other granddaughter plays soccer three times a week, Edmonton being the national centre for women's soccer.

I also wanted to get up to date on all things Alberta. Number one, the sales tax is 5%. Everyone knows it should be higher: the revenue is needed, but it would be political suicide for any leader to suggest that publicly. I toured the really beautiful new hockey rink, the Rogers Centre, with a sculpture of Wayne out front hoisting the Stanley Cup. I posed with Wayne and heard the story of the Centre.

The NHL brings huge pressure on cities which have hockey franchises to build bigger, better sites at public expense. Former Edmonton mayor Stephen Mandel resisted and took five years to broker a deal with the league to share costs.

The centre is all glass, curves and open space and has access to the LRT and an adjoining park.

Do you know that in neighbouring Calgary before the recent mayoral election (Naheed Nenshi won), Gary Bettman came to town to campaign against Nenshi, who is taking the same firm stand for his city.

I learned the bus system and made my way to West Edmonton Mall. The skating rink is being renovated so I wasn't able to take a turn at that. Sears is, alas, closing there too. I was in line to buy a cooking pot and got chatting with a young couple from Saskatchewan as I admired their chubby baby. When my turn came at the cash, this smiling young mother said to the clerk, "I have a leftover Sears credit for $2.50. Please apply it to this womans purchase."

Wow. From Saskatchewan to Ontario via Alberta. National Unity.

The second goodness story comes from Peterborough. There was a message on my machine when I got home. The talented craftsman-artist John Madill had read I was to give a public talk on November 14 on my Camino de Santiago pilgrimage in Spain. He wanted to give me a detailed model of the Cathedral in Santiago which he had built via the craft of card modelling, which is popular in Europe. It is a work of art, about 2 feet square, with two bell towers, a cloister, a clock tower and walls with flags that look like the setting for knights heading off to the Crusades. Each of the four facades opens on to a plaza. In four days there, I never did figure out which door opened onto which plaza.

All is made of paper, finely wrought, richly decorated, probably taking as many hours to make as the original medieval churches did. John has 50 such models in his home. He has given one of Peterborough St. Peters Cathedral to the bishop, and three to Trent University of their various buildings.

I have no doubt John's model will be the hit of my talk.

Small acts perhaps, but they lift one up. I am resolved to make pleasant small talk wherever I go in town. And no complaining. Nine out of 10 times, it is welcomed; service people moving groceries along, coffee servers wishing one a nice day, delivery men coming more than once.

Yes it's platitudinous, but perhaps the oil that will smooth a rough patch for someone, and contribute a little something to what is called quality of life in Peterborough.

Eat, Read, Think: By the Bridge and Books and Bodums November 23, 2017

There's a bit of a culinary/social/ literary movement going on over on Water Street near Hunter.

What many are calling the "best kept secret in town," the 30-seat restaurant, "By the Bridge," now three years old, and its adjoining book room, "Books and Bodums" is quietly having an impact on Peterborough's downtown, attracting the lunch crowd who value good food and "healthy choices" and who now, in an attached room, can sit quietly in easy chairs, browsing the extensive but not overwhelming, selection of contemporary books.

They can look over the Guardian Weekly, open up their laptops, sit in the sunny window and even think a little, detached from the hubbub of the workplace or the diners next door.

Not Starbucks in tone, but with much the same ambience for relaxation, the two spaces are drawing an increasing clientele: students, scholars, activists and downtown workers. Prices are modest: the space can be rented out to groups for small meetings, all on a sliding scale.

As the reputation for good food spreads, By the Bridge is doing more catering, getting orders via email and spending the early morning hours chopping and cooking and then readying for lunch.

The leader behind this two-sided creation, with a firm philosophy of what it is about, is owner Bridget Cullen, joined by a very well-informed staff.

Cullen, from Waterloo, took training in culinary arts at George Brown College in Toronto, and then served a two-year apprenticeship, followed by studies in Food and Nutrition Management.

"I loved to cook. My husband and I ate out in Toronto at various ethnic restaurants and tried making what we ate, from mu shoo pork to onion bajis. Here, I loved The Electric Clove and the Twilight Diner," she says.

Coming to Trent in 1998, Cullen took to the city and wanted to manage a restaurant, but with a family of four, also wanted a reasonable pace of life. By the Bridge is open 11 to 3, five days a week, and for some special events.

The original staff of two persons has grown to nine.

Cullen purchases fresh food from local sources. She rents the premises, and when the next-door space became available, she invested in renovating it as an attractive book nook.

"I love reading," she says. "I love the feel of books. One side of our enterprise is bustling, one side is calm. I also believe in trusting the community, the clients, the neighbours and the customers. It is way less stressful that way."

"We serve between 50 and 100 customers at lunch in person, and another 100-200 in the hours before that delivering food. We all work hard but our satisfaction is high."

The books are carefully chosen, to reflect the best of modern thinking on important topics. A few are donated. They are for sale.

"Our focus is on authors from different countries and Canadian writers who bring different perspectives to big issues that affect us all. I also favour award-winning books. Water Street used to be 'book lane' but we are the only bookstore left here now. We specialize in international development, climate issues, women's issues and poverty. Its our way of affecting changes in views and in policies," she says.

I browse the titles: Michael, Ondaatje, George Monbiot, David Suzuki, Jeffry Sachs, Malcom Gladwell, Miriam Toews, Paulo Coelho. I look at the posters; prominent is the one for the lecture on *Writing as Resistance* to be given November 20 by Pulitzer-prize-winning author and American journalist, Chris Hedges.

As Peterborough develops as a hub for students and active citizens who also appreciate a good salad, this friendly combo of eatery and library is filling the bill for more and more people.

It sings with good citizenship.

Between the Lines: the Power of Alternative Publishing December 7, 2017

I've been thinking quite a bit about the shape of leadership in a community these days.

With the collapse of the American dream, shattered into fragments of bitterness, violence and division, and an appalling leader, we to the North must get busy building up and strengthening an alternate society: civil, honest, frugal, respectful of Indigenous roots, deeply democratic and multi-cultural.

Much, much work to be done, many visions to dream, some sacrifice to endure. What kinds of leaders shall we follow, take cues from, emulate?

In a community such as Peterborough, there are the visible leaders: elected politicians, scarcely-known school trustees, highly-paid civil servants (administrators in health, education, and policing), companies and banks and business leaders.

But then there is another layer of almost invisible influencers: on-the-ground organizers such as Alan Slavin and Daphne Ingram; moral leaders such as Christian Harvey and Leo Coughlin, Elizabeth Rahman, Julie Stoneberg and Larry Gillman; NGO heads such as Brianna Salmon and Charmaine Magumbe; youth such as Kaia Douglas, Kristin Muskratt and Sneha Wadhwani; philanthropists such as Bill and Betty Morris; educators such as Joe Webster and Jacob Rodenberg; and writers such as Janette Platana and David Tough.

I salute them and their Canadian kind!

It all brings me to two people I consider powerhouses in the formation of conscience in this town: Ferne Cristall and Rob Clarke.

This column will focus on Rob. He grew up in Peterborough, went to Queen's, and was an original member, in 1977, of the alternative publishing house "Between the Lines," whose history he has just told in the graphic book, *Books without Bosses: 40 Years of Reading Between the Lines.*

Cristall and Clarke have been back in Peterborough since 1990. Rob, an editor and collective member of the "left wing" Toronto-based publishing house "Between the Lines," Ferne a teacher and long-time volunteer for the Reframe Film Festival.

Clarke's new book is a colourful, 53- page graphic novel, 8 by 11 inches, with a cover based on the Beatles record *Sergeant Pepper's Lonely Hearts Club Band.* It tells in comic book format, the story of "Between the Lines." It is wittily written and robustly illustrated by artist Kara Sievewright of Haida Gwai.

212

In a joint project of two entities, the Development Education Centre of Toronto (DEC) and Dumont Press Graphix of Kitchener, "a worker-owned and controlled typesetting and printshop" in the heady days of progressive thought of the 1970s, "Between the Lines" took as its mandate to publish non-fiction books by mostly Canadian authors on social and cultural issues, with non-mainstream viewpoints. It operated out of a United Church, St. Paul's Avenue Rd, which also housed Greenpeace and the Toronto Committee for the Liberation of South Africa.

It was a gadfly, which persistently challenged readers to re-think the world around them, asking uncomfortable questions. It did make some people uncomfortable: in 1976, the RCMP reported on DEC in its surveillance report.

BTL had no boss, no owner. it was a collective and has published over 300 influential books, the first one being *The Big Nickel: Inco at Home and Abroad* by Jamie Swift. That book sold at $5: print runs were usually 2000 copies.

Says Prof Fiona Jeffries of the University of Ottawa: "BTL does vital, radical cultural work bringing hidden histories to the surface." It has an unquenchable thirst for social change through the power of bookdom.

Authors have included Ursula Franklin, Mary Jo Leddy, Charlie Angus, Noam Chomsky, bell hooks, and Vandana Shiva.

"This has been a fairly good year," says Rob. "Full-time staff is now at four people, including Peterborough's Jenn Tiberio."

Rob Clarke's current project is writing *Packed to the Doors: Peterborough's Movie-Going History*, a story that begins in 1897 in the Bradburn Opera House.

Should be an eye-opener.

Website *www.peterboroughmoviehistory.com*

Speaking of a Stable for a Baby:
Peterborough's YES Shelter
December 21, 2017

I can't help thinking that Christmas/ Hanukkah/Kwanzaa is a time for concentration on the needy among us.

Homeless youth are high among them. For fifteen years on Brock Street, the YES Shelter for Youth and Families has stood, now with more pressure on it than ever. Its modest accommodation is not meeting the need for temporary housing for youth in crisis.

At present YES houses 15 youth, most in small double rooms, and 15 family members: parents/caregivers with children. Peterborough's vacancy rate for housing is less than 1%. Housing experts say a healthy rate in a community is 3%.

So the youth, almost all from our immediate area, ages 16-24, who are homeless because of poverty, abuse, family breakdown, addictions and mental health issues come to YES, and are supported by non-judgmental workers.

The shelter is humble, with narrow halls and a playroom and laundry in the basement. Nonetheless, it has a spirit of calm most days. There are many helpful staff and volunteers. Close links are kept with the police, with Fourcast, and with the schools. Out back at YES, there is the "Carriage House," where qualified teachers guide the youth in obtaining high school credits.

YES strives to have youth stay just six weeks, and great effort is made to find housing, either for a group or an individual. But due to the housing crisis, youth require more time in emergency housing. A housing support worker has recently been hired, who will work with willing landlords and youth tenants to solve problems.

Occupancy at YES has increased 64% over five years.

Executive Director Meagan La Plante, who succeeded the respected Suzanne Galloway last summer, along with Board Chair Wendy Love, are quick to point to assistance they receive from the Peterborough community. Red Lobster faithfully delivers food each week. Home Depot on Lansdowne has a highly motivated staff, who come to paint and repair the shelter, and have been cheerfully asking every customer at the store for a donation to YES.

The annual budget at YES is around $750,000, much self-raised.

One dedicated volunteer has been sorting donated clothes at YES for years. YES has a volunteer driver, and students from Fleming College social work studies come to help. It is also the beneficiary of funds from an event organized by the opposite end of the spectrum, the Trent Fashion Society. The Peterborough 360 Clinic, headed by insightful nurse Kathy Hardill, looks to the youth's health needs.

TASS (inspired by teacher Jeff Bergeron), Kenner and St Peter's high schools are important donors. (As an further positive aside, I was in St Peter's recently and heard a PA announcement asking for donations of feminine hygiene products for Crossroads and YES. Bags and bags came in. They were delivered to the sites by young men students). Megan Hennessy was named volunteer of the year at YES.

Those are Christmas stories to tell my grandchildren.

"Most homeless adults," says Meagan, "start out as homeless youth. We try to break the cycle. The youth here are resilient and capable. I work in this field because I know when we support youth they move on to do incredible things."

Wendy, who grew up in Goderich and worked in the Ontario public service in corrections before retirement, agrees. "It's hard work," she says, "and one see some awful things at times. Homeless youth sometimes take their own lives. But it is very rewarding."

Some groups are over-represented in the homeless population: Indigenous youth and LGBTQ2 youth. The public school board in March 2016 reported that 32 students were homeless. This Christmas/Hanukkah/Kwanzaa season, we Canadians are spending $6 billion dollars on gifts and travel. We might also look closely around home, and critically at the expenditure meant to honour these feasts.

Annual report at *www.yesshelter.ca*

Reform Comes Agonizingly Slow
January 4, 2018

I once again take up the topic of reform in the Catholic church, because I'm a kind of an insider/outsider, a Pope-watcher, and an analyst who knows the immense power and global reach of this church. And the sad effects of its mistaken teachings and practices.

There were two items in recent news: one the death of American Cardinal Bernard Law of Boston, age 86, who, after being indicted on charges related to his cover-up of clergy sex abuse against children, fled to Rome in 2002 and was put in charge of a major church. Remember the courageous journalism of the *Boston Globe* and the subsequent film *Spotlight*.

Here is what Canadian politician Charlie Angus, NDP MP from Cobalt, Ontario, had to say in an anguished post:

"I learned my lessons in faith and justice in the church. I remember pastors organizing over the grape boycott for farmworkers. I was working at a Catholic Worker house when the sexual abuse scandals first came to light. They were stunning revelations, but even more stunning was to see powerful men who were supposed to follow the words of Jesus suppress, cover-up and protect serial predators. Cardinal Law was eventually brought down by a grand jury indictment, but protected by Pope John Paul II. He was a disgrace to everything Jesus stood for. Good riddance."

In Canada, we had our own searing scandal at Mount Cashel orphanage in Newfoundland 40 years ago, where 300 young persons alleged physical and sexual abuse by the Christian Brothers, cover-up by churchmen and police collusion.

The Newfoundland government ordered an inquiry and the report in 1992 by former lieutenant-governor Gordon Winter caused the Archbishop, Alphonsus Penney to resign, the orphanage to be closed and razed, some priests to go to jail and the churches largely to be emptied.

The second item has just been a bombshell of a report from Australia on sex abuse of children, years after the Canadian report. It is a mind-boggling 17 volumes, the result of a five-year study undertaken when Julia Gillard was Prime Minister. Australia has 25 million people, of whom 5 million are Catholic. Catholic personnel, mostly priests and brothers, have been found responsible for 62% of the 4,444 cases of child sex abuse committed in the years 1950-2009. The report described Church behaviour as a "catastrophic failure of leadership."

Among its 400 recommendations are ones asking the church to change its requirement for clerical celibacy, and another asking for relaxation of the confessional seal of secrecy where incidents of children and abuse are involved. Fairly radical, but they seem to me reasonable.

In Rome? The Pontifical Commission for the Protection of Children has just lost a woman member, Marie Collins, a survivor from Ireland, who resigned and said the Vatican has not put in the resources needed to enforce policies. "I have watched events unfold with dismay," she said. "There are still men in Vatican who resist work to help children."

Pope Francis strives mightily to change the culture and to institute reform. He is undermined by several curial members. Still and all, with whatever personnel, the structures of the church endure, and are at the root.

The exclusion of women from all offices of the Catholic church, the grip of conservative elderly celibate men, and a backward sexual ethic which will not even withdraw the ban on contraception, leave one doubtful about the future of the institution.

The website for the Peterborough Catholic diocese says in a 17-page policy called *Clergy Abuse Reporting Guidelines*, adopted in 2011, that no child is to be alone with a priest, and preparation for childhood sacraments must be done in a group setting.

It makes woeful reading for the New Year. But now it is open and out there, and provides data for the faithful to use as they lobby for major changes.

Market Hall: the Downtown Miracle January 11, 2018

When I look back at my best moments of 2017, those having to do with mind and spirit, many involve experiences at our own Market Hall.

The one under the now-accurate town clock.

Soaring and classical, whose beautiful picture filled five columns in the January 2 Examiner, a building built for farmers in 1889, Market Hall is thriving, in the black, and now with an identity that means fewer and fewer people are asking: "Market Hall? Exactly where is that?"

I went to the Morrison lecture at the beginning of the year, with the eminent Cambridge economist Ha Joon Chang, whose talk was a mental stretch for me. He is an encyclopedic global thinker, but with an affable personality. There were the plays brought here by Randy Read of New Stages, the "page on the stage" series, satisfying, often new, Canadian work, which, when read after one run-through by trained actors, transport the audience to settings through imagination. My fav is Rick Roberts of CBC TV when he comes.

Affordability? Randy Read's series costs $100 for five plays. The Morrison lecture is free. There was the inspiring *In From the Cold* concert, my first-ever, presented by the group, "Carried Away" led by musicians John Hoffman, Sue Newman and Rob Fortin.

A benefit, with talent and generosity.

For years, "Folk under the Clock' has delighted patrons with the best of folk music. Performers uniformly rave about this performance space with its intimate vibe, (from 220-to 320 seats), its sloping roof and first-class acoustics. We are talking Diana Krall, Great Big Sea, and Serena Ryder.

Not to mention free downtown parking evenings at the King Street lot.

In October, there was the stimulating, highly personal talk by a longstanding leftist hero of mine, Chris Hedges.

Chris Hedges to Peterborough: how can that be? He is a Pulitzer prize-winning journalist and writer, with a divinity degree from a Presbyterian seminary. Turns out, in a delicious revelation, Chris Hedges is a boyhood friend of Bill Kimble, who is a longtime cultural leader in Peterborough, now of Public Energy. The two of them had edited an underground paper in high school.

Bill Kimball figures largely in this story. To get it, I sought out my old teaching colleague from St. Peter's, Charlie Werger, and took him to coffee. It seems that 20 years ago, the Toronto-based corporation that owned Peterborough Square and the attached Market Hall, was about to convert the hall into a bingo hall. (It had, in the fifties, been a badminton court).

Kimball formed a citizens committee, made up of Charlie, his spouse, Jane Werger, Rob Steinman and a few others. They managed to talk the corporation out of this plan, and got the City of Peterborough to buy Market Hall.

They formed a non-profit organization called Market Hall Performing Arts, got incorporated in 1998, and set about, first of all, to clean the place, paint, and clean washrooms. They pay rent to the City, receive a City grant of about $35,000 a year and can issue tax receipts for donations. It became clear in 2010 that the Hall needed major renovations, and all three levels of government pitched in. A beautiful result.

Charlie has volunteered at Market Hall Performing Arts Inc. for 20 straight years. He is for me, a model of a person who found joy and meaning in his working life, and on retirement carried right on volunteering in the arts, loving the local and international fare.

"Oh, and a favorite place now for weddings," he smiles.

There is a dynamic General Manager, Chad Hogan, a musician with business credentials, a good website and plans to expand *Market Hall Presents* shows.

It is a jewel, and will be celebrated Friday, January 12, with a *Lights Up* show. $20. *website www.markethall.org*

A Visionary Hopes to Return Land: Janice Keil
January 18, 2018

Three years ago, a dynamic woman, a retiring teacher, Janice Keil, age 59, chose to relocate to Peterborough from Toronto. She had done research, looking for a small city that had a good cycling infrastructure and a progressive cultural/ political community.

We qualified.

Clear-eyed about her goals and values, with prodigious energy, she moved ahead: found an apartment on Charlotte Street and plunged in to her projects - setting up a design for a feminist construction project to build a passive solar house near Campbellford. (In season she cycles out there, having no car. That's about a five-hour cycle.)

It is meant to be a training module, with crews of women building affordable housing to the EU Passivhaus standard.

But more, Janice spent seven years finding and buying 97.3 acres of land in Northumberland County, because she now intends to make her contribution to reconciliation with Indigenous people by returning this land to Alderville First Nation on the south shore of Rice lake.

That has made national news. In an October 22, 2017 interview, Janice told Rebecca Deerchild of CBC radio's *Unreserved* about her hope and the reasons behind it. Janice who is very articulate, explained her determination to respond to the recommendations of the recently-concluded Truth and Reconciliation Report in a personal way.

Responses poured in to Deerchild's program from across Canada. "Interestingly," says Janice, "most were from women. They spoke of their shoreline and other holdings: of their conscience and new awareness, and of their desire to take real action."

Along with a friend, Ian Attridge, a Peterborough lawyer who specializes in land trust work, Janice called on the chief of Alderville, Jim-Bob Marsden and band council in the territory on October 20, 2017.

The leaders were interested and appreciative. One of their concerns was the implications of taxation in following years. They promised to visit the land in the spring, have a blessing and a celebratory meal. The acreage doesn't abut the Alderville land, but is about 30 km away.

Janice agrees there is much to be worked out. In the U.S. there is a structure called the Indigenous Land Trust which enables such "gifts" to be made. One of her hopes is that this will give rise to a similar organization in Canada. But Janice is quick to point out the problems with the language at present.

"This is not a 'gift,' she observes. "A gift is something that is given freely. Even though I have a piece of paper called a deed, the land was not originally 'given' in any sense. This is a repatriation or return."

A deep ecologist, Janice tell me she camps on her land (there is no building), and listens to nature as a motivation for her initiative. Bobolinks and Eastern meadowlarks are her companions. "The land is tall grass prairie," she says.

Janice grew up on a farm north on London ON and went to the University of Western Ontario, and to the University of Waterloo, gaining an M.A. in German Studies. Subsequently, since she had an interest in theology, she earned a Master of Divinity at Regis College U. of T. She has many friends who sustain her faith and activism.

"It is forging a new path," she says, "making the path by going. There is no template, no legal precedent. No one knows more about the land and water that Indigenous people. We must learn and learn quickly."

She continues: "The next 150 years will determine who we Canadians really are. Land is central to everything about reconciliation. I am 60 years old. I would love to have this settled by the time I am 80!"

The Quilting Way of Kindness
February 8, 2018

Five years ago, my spouse of 52 years passed from this life in the peace and quiet of the Palliative Care Unit of PRHC.

My son and I kept vigil for three days, and on John's last day, 19 friends and colleagues and neighbours came by for a quiet word. I think some of them were whispering they would do their best to keep me from making big mistakes in the future without his advice.

It was all we could have hoped for, as his long and heroic life ended. But there was one more heartfelt comfort for us.

John had been covered by a bright and colourful handmade quilt, maroon and white. Son Paul folded it and went to return it to the desk.

"No, sir," said the nurse softly. "That is for you and your family. The Kawartha Quiltmakers Guild donates them to this Unit and to the sick children's ward too."

Two weeks later, I wrote a note to these anonymous quilters to thank them for such a sensitive and meaningful gift. When I took it to Palliative Care the nurse said, "How nice. These folks receive very few responses. They just carry on."

At that moment I decided to write about the group at some point.

This week I interviewed Cathy Vickers, a master quilter, member of the Kawartha Guild and honoured quilter at the annual show, May 4, 5, and 6 at the Mount Community Centre. Cathy took first prize in the Guild Rosette competition in 2016 for her quilt *Free Spirit*. Her work will also be on display at the National Juried Show in Toronto this year.

The oldest existing quilt in Canada dates back to 1810. It is currently exhibited at a museum in Nova Scotia. "No thread in Canadian history is stronger or more consistent than the use of quilts as links between women and their descendants," said expert Pauline Grondin of Halton. "They express creativity and individuality."

The steady donation of finished quilts here to persons in distress is a story of quiet generosity and fidelity to a cause. The Millbrook Needlers, founded in 2012, with 60 members, provides quilts to Centennial Place in their village, as well as to Community Care and Children's Aid clients and the far-north communities.

"Smiles are bright on all sides," says past-president Elaine Young. "Our members desire that a little comfort and warmth be brought to others."

Linda Lawrence is an active member and reports that in 2017, 75 quilts were delivered from her group.

The Buckhorn Guild has donated to such charities as the hospital, the Breakfast Program for Buckhorn Public School and Kawartha Food Share. The coordinator is Georgean Morden.

What is given by these dozens of quilters in our region is time, fabric, talent and expense. A small quilt is worth at least $150. Concern and kindness have no price. Some members prepare a kit for others to complete.

Most quilters groups meet monthly and many oftener. The social benefits are easily seen.

Quilts were first made in Canada in the late 18th century, largely for warmth on the frontier. Children's clothes were cut down from those of elders. Top and bottom layers are cotton or wool and the filling in between is cotton or wool fibres.

The three layers are held together in a pre-decided pattern of even-running stitches sewn by hand or occasionally by machine.

Traditional patterns handed down from generation to generation include Log Cabin, Lone Star, Dresden and the double wedding rings.

Fabric artists today have books, workshops, websites and conferences. Some sell their work and take commissions. Some large national shows have drawn 50,000 people.

At the May Peterborough show, people can bring a quilt they value and have it appraised.

At the rate these guilds are covering us, we may all have a handmade quilt to enjoy some day.

Mental Health for All
February 22, 2018

As I crossed the lobby of the Trent Athletic Centre recently on my way to the warmest place in town, the sauna, I was struck by 43 poster-size messages prominent on the cement walls. In varying handwritten styles, they were messages of encouragement from students to fellow students who feel blue.

It was indeed "Bell Let's Talk Day," January 31, which is a huge public program, corporately sponsored, with widespread advertising and an offer to donate 5 cents to mental health programs for every text, tweet or phone call sent on the Bell network. A table of young volunteers stood waiting for passersby to come and write. The writers were lined up.

Here are some signs that made me think:

"Don't be ashamed of your story; it will help others."

"We're all in this together. You are never alone."

"Use your privilege to give space and voice to someone who needs it."

"It's OK not to be OK."

"Someone says, suck it up - I say, huddle up."

"How are you? I will listen."

"If today all you did was hold yourself together, I'm proud of you."

And one student had remembered the words of Dr. Seuss.

"Today you are you, that is truer than true; there is no one alive who is youer than you."

Depression, mild and severe, is widely experienced across Canada right now. It's been a very cold, long winter of reduced light; of personal relations getting strained, of walking in slush, all of it endured in a world seemingly unhinged. Plugged in, we know too about too much grief, stupidity and threat. John Doyle, in the *Globe and Mail* says that we want to "retreat from a frightening and out-of-shape present."

There no better time to focus on mental health, how it is achieved and how it is maintained, says Kerri Davies of the local CMHA. "Loneliness is the new heart disease."

I asked her for some figures. Six million Canadians, about one in five, sought mental health help in 2017. Locally, the Canadian Mental Health Association serves four counties (Peterborough, Pine Ridge, Kawartha Lakes, Haliburton) on a $12 million budget with some 200 employees. The Four County Crisis program served 4500 individuals and responded to 2000 contacts each month.

But shortage of resources is key, says Davies. "Our budget from the province of $12 million has not increased in 8 years, yet more people are seeking help." The Ministry of Health allocates only 6% of its $54 billion to mental health services. Wait time for a person with an addiction or mental problem to see a professional is 1 to 3 months, down from 18 months last November.

"Through a partnership with PRHC, we have access to three new psychiatrists," she added. "We are encouraged."

Still, a long wait. The CMHA has launched an awareness campaign called "Erase the Difference" ahead of the provincial election in June.

Statistics show that youth, ages 15-24, suffer mood disorders and substance abuse problems more than any other age group. CMHA is especially proud of its Assertive Outreach Suicide Prevention program, located at the Peterborough and Lindsay hospitals.

Through it, 100 persons who made a serious attempt to end their lives have been helped and none has made a further attempt.

Sports figures such as Mike Babcock and Michael Landsberg are helping erase stigma, especially among men.

Local organizations such as Team55, Merrett Home Hardware and Herod Financial Services are crucial partners with CMHA.

Through donor-funded education last year, 232 educational sessions were given and eight thousand school children had mental health presentations. Hundreds have taken Mental Health First Aid, and a group program to support caregivers called *Journeying Together* is available.

Four out of five Canadian have recently reported they are more aware than they were of mental health. Good news.

Peterborough could become a hub for awareness, prevention and service.

Summer Jobs and "Attestations"
March 8, 2018

There has been a small but intense public dust-up over the insertion of a statement into applications for federal funding for student summer jobs by groups and agencies.

They must assert respect for the values underlying the Canadian Charter of Rights and Freedoms. Subtext: no work is to be undertaken by summer students who are federally funded, that would undermine reproductive rights or LGBT rights. Of these two, abortion is the neuralgic one, especially for a few Catholics and their leaders.

This required statement is new. Since 2010, 285 anti-choice groups in Canada have received $1.7 million in grants for summer jobs for students, and no accountability has been required to show they didn't use the money to advance their ideological agenda.

The Charter assures the right to equal treatment for minorities, including sexual minorities, and to reproductive rights, including abortion.

Seems straightforward enough. A government so committed to equality rights can hardly be expected to fund activities that would undermine them.

The ferocity of accusations against the Employment Minister Patti Hajdu, and Prime Minister Trudeau that they repress freedom of religion and impose views, reveals deep self-interest and hypocrisy.

Remember the odious bus ads sponsored by the Calgary-based Centre for Bio-Ethical Reform that we had to endure in Peterborough? They demonized abortion and the women, usually young and vulnerable, who sought them. That group received funding in the past.

Some "faith-based" religious groups are charging discrimination. The Roman Catholic bishop of Peterborough called on adherents to call the MP's office to protest.

I was a Vatican 11 Catholic in the heady days of the sixties and we naïve reformers expected major changes in the position of women in the church, followed by newly enlightened policies on birth control, homosexuality and abortion.

That was not to be, with Pope John XXIII followed by two conservative pontiffs. It seemed as if abortion was becoming the number one moral issue for Catholics worldwide: not poverty, not environmental destruction, not violence. The history of abortion theology and policy in the Church was not being taught anywhere in a fair-minded way.

When I was warned in the eighties not to raise the issue of abortion while teaching English at St. Peters Secondary School, I became curious, and was helped by the vigorous non-government organization in Washington called "Catholics for Choice."

Their research, publications and advocacy have literally changed the minds of legislatures around the world, especially in Catholic countries.

The absolutism about abortion endures in official circles, seminaries, schools, pontifical colleges, motherhouses and so on. This means the clergy class is woefully uninformed and the parish faithful are left to find out.

Against this backdrop, I lament the current fight against the summer jobs statement and Catholic leadership in it.

Enlightenment makes its way however, in many ways and places. Today in Canada, Catholics' opinion regarding the morality of abortion mirrors that of their neighbours: almost 80% are satisfied with the present situation and convinced of the importance of conscience in personal decision-making.

In 2015, the feminist and pro-choice Liberal government was elected. It has shown a firmness in all departments on the issue of protecting and enhancing the status of women. On the summer jobs issue, Minister Hajdu issued clarifying guidelines and examples.

An organization with anti-abortion beliefs applies for funding to hire students to serve meals to the homeless. It is eligible.

A "faith-based" organization that holds to the traditional definition of marriage as between one man and one woman hires students to deliver programs to reduce isolation among seniors. It is eligible but would be required to offer programs to all, regardless of sexual orientation or gender identity.

A summer camp applies to hire students as camp counsellors. As a camp that does not welcome LGBTQ2 youth, it is not eligible.

Seems like common sense to me. Human rights in law and in practice.

"Come From Away" Delights
March 22, 2018

I've been in some pretty risky situations in my life, such as moving to Kingston, Jamaica in the seventies just as the city was put under martial law, or moving to Dar es Salaam, Tanzania in 1978, just before Idi Amin invaded from Uganda. (We pushed him back, by the way).

But nothing compares with the risk of descending the steps of Upper Balcony B at the Royal Alexandra Theatre in Toronto. I don't know what the pitch of the balcony is, but it's not designed for me, the railings widely-spaced apart.

Still, it was well worth the adventure last week to see the stunning musical comedy-drama *Come From Away*.

It is not a Heritage Moment, such as we have all come to know and love, but 100 heritage moments, with no intermission. It is a dazzling display by 12 actors playing multiple roles, all with quick changes of accent: (Newfoundland or Texan or Middle Eastern), and rapid changes of character by means of a vest or a hat or a prayer rug.

It recreates the days after 9/11 when 38 planes filled with passengers from all over the world, 6000 traumatized people, landed in Gander, Newfoundland, a town of some 6000. So widespread was the fear of another attack, air space in North America was closed to traffic for five days.

Writers Irene Sankoff and David Hein, a Toronto husband-and-wife team, knew there was a story to discover here. So they went to the Rock and interviewed widely. Then they met the only female pilot to be stranded, Beverley Bass of American Airlines, and knew they had their pivot person.

Entirely sung, with a rousing eight-person back-up band, yes, a fiddle and accordion, *Come From Away* takes two perspectives: that of the stranded passengers, longing to get home or at least get off the plane, frantically connecting with family, and the viewpoint of the Gander community members.

Twelve astonishingly talented actors, of all ages and colours, have mastered the Newfoundland accent. The humour is deep and frequent. The rotund mayor already has a problem, even before the arrival of 6000 reluctant visitors. His bus drivers are on strike. He begs them to come back to work since there are hundreds of people to be carried around.

"My Corolla holds four," says one helpful citizen. The drivers relent just for this emergency.

Beulah has the juicy role of the "den mother," arranging mounds of food, island fare. One passenger asks ruefully, "Don't Canadians eat vegetables?" Beulah sends volunteers to the drugstore to get diapers and feminine hygiene products.

"In Frankfurt, Germany, it is four a.m.," she says cheerily to her team. "That's breakfast time - so go cook up the eggs!" She also befriends a worried New York mother, who actually, when it is all over, finds out her son has died in the towers.

Careful staging and creative lighting transform the revolving stage into an airliner, the Gander community hall, and a bar. A Newfy "screech-in" is held, the cod is kissed. The mayor, with an idea for some really Canadian recreation, instructs an African-American to "go to all the backyards and collect brooms." The lad falters. "I'll get shot," he says.

One of my heartiest laughs came when a sweet young Newfoundlander, resplendent in a WALMART jacket, sees a weary, dishevelled passenger. "Welcome to WALMART!" And then more softly, "Would you like to come home for a shower?"

A smash hit on Broadway, *Come from Away* had its best moment when playing at the Gander Community Centre Hockey Rink, where a standing ovation started ten minutes before the end of the play. The cost? The face of my ticket said $30, but I had bought a series of seven Mirvish matinees this year. The GO bus and train was $19.65 same day return.

The experience: priceless.

This Global Gig Deepens
March 29, 2018

It seems as if, ready or not, I am to serve on this fascinating new project introduced by Prime Minister Trudeau, who has called together a group of 19 persons from 12 countries, 18 women and one Canadian man, to prepare advice for the G7 leaders on gender equality in today's world.

Its called the Gender Equality Advisory Council. No pay, but six months of interactions with heroic women.

In 2018, the idea of radical equality has come around again with new force and urgency. Heavens, in Beijing at the United Nations Conference on Women way back in 1995, I heard the cry "Look at the World Through Women's Eyes."

The seven leaders of the democracies (Italy, France, Germany, the UK , the US, Japan and Canada) come to Charlevoix, Quebec, June 8 and 9 for their annual meeting. Since Canada is host this year it sets the agenda. Mr Trudeau, who is an ardent feminist, wants to increase gender commitment from his colleagues in the G7 under four headings: economics and employment, violence and conflict, sexual matters, and climate justice.

So, some of the 19 who came to New York last week to attend the 62nd annual meeting of the Commission on the Status of Women at the UN, met up to begin work. They are, every one, accomplished, brave and well-known. No feminist says "no" to our prime minister when called on these days. We all see the opportunity in this moment in time to give the progress of women, and therefore of humanity, a push.

I have to tell you there are two Nobel Laureates in the group (Liberia and Pakistan), one managing director of the IMF, one Canadian ambassador to France, one famous feminist economist who created the term "gender based budgeting," one head of OXFAM Uganda, one head of the YWCA of Canada, and a Dane who is head of the NGO "Women Deliver."

There is also Melinda Gates of the Gates Foundation in Seattle, which has 1500 employees and access to $40 billion.

Then there is me. Don't tell me you don't notice a certain gap. I don't have a smart phone, I have no staff, and my printer is very tired.

But I do have two major strengths.

One is the support of my community. There's been an outpouring of enthusiasm and congratulations to greet my appointment in Peterborough and the Kawarthas. I have received 250 messages of encouragement, fully 40% from men. (Of course, having 3 sons helps that proportion.) We won't get too far without the engagement of men. I laughed when Aex Neve, executive director of Amnesty International, wrote, "Watch out, world," and had all the staff, anglophone and francophone, sign it.

So, after I get the autographs of my sister committee members, I will get to work with them. We need to be bold and produce a strong statement for the leaders to consider, and we hope, adopt. It needs to be fact-laden, pithy and short. I remember Prime Minister Jean Chretien saying to his staff: "This is a very complex issue: I don't want more than one page on it!"

We will seek some accountability. If it can't be measured it won't happen.

The second strength I have is where I come from. This area is resource-rich with brains, commitment, goodwill, and a profound desire to make a better world. I will consult with Al and Linda Slavin, Julia Anderson and Prof Haroon-Akram Lodhi, with Green Up, and with Kaitlyn Ittermann of Sustainable Peterborough.

I chose the Working Group "gender and climate justice."

Already, activists and scholars from Peterborough are in touch. If I look bad for Peterborough on the world stage, it won't be the fault of my consultants.

I plan to keep readers informed of this adventure all the way.

Two Canadian Women Take New York by Storm
April 12, 2018

I visited the Big Apple recently, the first time in 20 years. What I saw were two Canadian women taking the town by storm, each in difference sectors.

I was hanging out with an Inuk woman, President Rebecca Kudloo of the Inuit Women of Canada (Pauktuutit), from Baker Lake in Nunavut, and with the head of the Metis women of Canada, Melanie Omeniho. They were part of our delegation to the annual UN Conference on Women. They were such fun to be with: speaking poignantly about their groups, tipping cabbies lavishly ("they have families to support") and making an impression everywhere with their authenticity. They wanted to see a Broadway musical, and I was game.

Ten blocks from our hotel was Times Square, and there at the Stephen Sondheim Theatre, the musical about the life of American songwriter Carole King was playing to sold-out crowds. King had written over 100 hit songs in the sixties, including *You've Got a Friend*.

Here's the Canadian connection: the show, called *Beautiful* stars Chilina Kennedy of Toronto, formerly of Stratford and Shaw, a demon of a piano player and singer, who rightfully earns a standing ovation every night.

Here's another New York story: at intermission, naturally, the line-up for the men's washroom is short; for the women's, long. The usher calls out briskly, "Ladies, pee with purpose, please!" We did our best to comply.

Some 12 or 14 blocks away on the East River, the impressive United Nations compound reaches to the sky.

Here, Peterborough's Maryam Monsef, Minister of Status of Women, was head of the Canadian delegation, some 200 people, who had come to the 62nd annual UN Commission on Women meeting.

We were from civil society organizations who work with women, civil servants, elected MPs and MPPs, Cabinet Ministers, and staff from the Canadian Mission to the UN who were our affable hosts all week. At one reception, Monsef had us navigate to a part of the room for our sector, then find a person from another group, and spend five minutes catching up. I nailed Speaker of the House, Geoff Regan. "You do a good job," I told him. A maritimer, with the usual sense of humour, Regan answered, "My wife thinks so."

Monsef's ease at hosting, and her friendly, down-to-earth style make her easy to relate to, and fosters community. Then, her formidable intellect readies her to deliver up to four speeches a day on different topics. I was there and I saw it. This is not a political piece, it is a paean of praise from an older woman to a gifted younger one.

One morning, she addressed a breakfast meeting of 600 people from around the world on engaging men and boys in the work of progress for women. A little later, it was a keenly-received speech on accountability for civil society organizations in receipt of money from any source, along with a helpful handout prepared by Canadian John Reed that was quickly snapped up, especially by reps from developing countries.

Then on to a lunch talk on gender-based budgeting with Finance Minister Bill Morneau, and finally a rousing five-minute speech in the General Assembly on Canada's progress in gender equality. Canadian commitment now is widely praised at the UN as global leadership par excellence.

All this without flagging, Monsef with a certain grace and simplicity.

Peterborough can take pride in its member, who has risen to national and international leadership based on her talent and goodness.

At the opening session in the General Assembly, the Secretary General of the UN Antonio Guterres of Portugal, proclaimed "I am a feminist" to prolonged applause. Sadly, American women are demoralized and almost invisible.

Then there was St. Patrick's Day, as only New York can do it. I found a Mass in Gaelic that morning, and the pubs opened at nine.

Nunavut and Peterborough's Judge April 19, 2018

How is it that until recently I knew so little about this vast, sparsely populated, but important Canadian territory?

In the last two weeks, I have chatted with an Inuk woman, Rebecca Kudloo, who heads the Inuit Women's Organization of Canada (Pauktuuitit), and I have had coffee with Mr. Justice Alan Ingram, the Peterborough family court justice who is spending several weeks a year in court in Nunavut communities.

It has been an education.

Nunavut is made up of 100 large islands and 36,000 smaller ones comprising 2 million square kilometres of land and water - 21% of the total area of Canada. Almost all of it is above 60 degrees, above the tree line, and therefore Arctic tundra.

Winter can bring 24 hours of dark, and summer 24 hours of light.

Nunavut has a population of just under 40,000 people (85% Inuit) in its 26 scattered communities, none of which are connected by road.

It was carved out of the Northwest Territories in 1999, after 16 years of negotiation with the Government of Canada. It has a deep desire to become self-reliant, keeping its languages, customs and way of life.

The capital is Iqaluit, a town of 9,000 on Baffin Island, where the Territorial Legislature has 22 members and a Premier, Paul Quassa. For representation in Ottawa, there is one Nunavut MP and one Nunavut Senator. The hubs are Iqaluit, Rankin Inlet and Baker Lake. (Baker Lake, with 2000 persons, is where Rebecca Kudloo lives.)

What takes Justice Ingram there? Volunteering, and following a passion for indigenous people and the north, first fostered when as a student he spent summers leading tours to the Yukon and NWT, and later lived on the Nipissing Reserve near Sturgeon Falls.

After thirty-one years as a judge in Peterborough, he learned about the opportunity to serve Canada's north. A few southern judges have been authorized to assist the local judges with their workload.

As more Inuit lawyers are being trained, he expects to see more Inuit judicial appointments in the future. In the north he travels on circuits, on small aircraft with the crown attorney, interpreters, defence lawyers and court staff.

Court may be held in arenas, community centres and school halls.

When in court, he sits with an Inuit elder and two Inuktitut interpreters. The offences are of a criminal nature: drug use, domestic assault. Each community has an RCMP detachment.

Ingram prepared for this assignment by reading northern cases and history, including Peterborough writer Shelagh Grant's *Arctic Justice*, and following the daily *Nunatsiak News*.

There are painful problems in Nunavut: climate change, poverty, unemployment and health. 10% of the people have tuberculosis, and one community, Qikiqtarjuak, was recently closed to outsiders.

But the whole territory has internet, and there is a college providing teaching and nursing training. There is a growing number of Inuit taking leadership positions, southerners who have adopted it as home, and a surprising number of hard-working immigrants.

Ingram tries to deliver sentences that are culturally appropriate. Recently he sentenced a convicted offender to "Go on a seal hunt, kill a seal and distribute the meat to the village elders." He ordered one offender to regularly take his medication for tuberculosis.

Last year's Reframe Festival featured a documentary "Angry Inuk" on a successful Inuit designer who uses sealskin for beautiful products.

Alan Ingram loves the land, flying in when the pilot himself turns on the runway lights. He enjoys the hospitality of the people, going out on an ATV or having meals in a home. On off-hours, he walks the community, and always stops at the Food Bank.

It was easy to sense the feeling of enthusiasm in yet another Peterburian giving national service.

As we left the coffee shop, Alan Ingram said to the cashier, "Go north, young man."

I salute the spirit of the judge.

Marjorie Hogg Burns with daughter
Rosemary and son Peter, Kirkland Lake 1937

My Mother, My Heroine
May 10, 2018

This year on Mother's Day, I will be hailing in some wonderment, the life of Marjorie Hogg Burns, my mother.

Her life of 83 years, spent entirely in the District of Temiskaming, a three-hour drive north of North Bay, she would think unremarkable. But my perspective and the facts show otherwise.

Her father, Samuel Hogg from Cobourg, had homesteaded to the north in 1897. Arriving in New Liskeard and finding all the Crown lands along the Wabi River recorded, he went 12 miles away to locate his farm. He walked to the foot of Lake Temiskaming to a mill for lumber, built a punt and slept under it, while trees were being cut and a little shack built.

In June 1898, Sam Hogg returned to Baltimore, Ontario for his bride, Alberta Mitchell, who was welcomed to the north in a canoe decorated with wild flowers.

She wrote at the time, "For my first few years in this new land, the torture suffered by mosquitoes and black flies was my most trying experience."

Ministers from New Liskeard came to the settlement, now called Milberta, for an occasional service. These circuit riders came by horse and stayed over at my mother's childhood home. The school house opened in 1899 with nine pupils. A first child, Alexander, was born in 1900, and my mother in 1904. Samuel Hogg was elected first Reeve of the Township.

There are gaps in my mother's story. I regret not asking her more fully. I know she won a public speaking contest in 1917 from the Canada Victory Loan Competition. I have the medal: she was 13 years old.

Then she went to North Bay Normal School at age 17, and the next year was teaching in a one-room schoolhouse, Whitewood Grove in Hilliard Township. She would have been 18.

The dreadful Haileybury forest fire occurred in 1922, over two days. There were 54 deaths. It swept through 650 square miles.

The curator of the Haileybury museum wrote to me in 2004.

"Your mother, Miss Marjorie Hogg, protected the school children by shepherding them under a small bridge and keeping soaked blankets around them. When the smoke and fire seemed to be advancing rapidly, she had made some trunk calls to parents. 'Wait, I'll run outside and look' said one. The parent came back to the phone and had time to say, 'Don't dismiss them: we are cut off by the fire.' The line went dead. If Miss Hogg had dismissed the class, very few would have reached home alive."

Her parent's home in New Liskeard was destroyed and within it, her hope chest full of embroidered items, her trousseau.

Twelve years later, she was principal of Kirkland West School in Kirkland Lake. A young Catholic lawyer from Almonte, Ontario arrived in town. My mother had been courted by many young mining engineers who had come in the gold rush, but she chose my father. The religious tensions, Catholic and Protestant of the time, prevented them, now in their thirties, from marrying there, so they went to Toronto.

My father seems to have established the religion of the household, so we four kids were raised Catholic. My mother, the onetime Methodist organist, told me once she never had put her "whole weight" down in that church.

She was a cultured woman who played the piano for memorable family sing-songs, a great cook whose specialty was cheese straws, and a legendary bridge player. She encouraged me to read, play sports, and run for student council. She suffered a long, undiagnosed illness stoically.

Into our home came her elderly, hearing-impaired mother.

Next year, I hope to honour my mother and my Scots Presbyterian heritage, by joining Reverend Bob Root on a pilgrimage to the Church of Scotland mission on the island of Iona in the Hebrides.

We are blessed when we have had strong, loving and gracious mothers.

Rosemary Ganley with women from across Canada and Minister of Status of Women Monsef, at the UN in New York, March, 2018

Epilogue

These columns represent my thinking over a recent four-year period. I hope that thinking continues to expand and be open to change and new ideas. Readers, their work and their convictions, have greatly affected my perspective. Let's carry on.

About Rosemary Ganley

Rosemary Ganley is a Peterborough-based writer and journalist. Born in Kirkland Lake, Ontario, she studied English and philosophy at the University of Toronto, and taught secondary school for many years in Cornwall, ON, Dorval, PQ, and Peterborough, ON in public, separate and independent schools.

In 1975, she and her spouse John Ganley and their three young boys accepted a teaching assignment in Kingston, Jamaica through the Canadian International Development Agency. Their lives were changed. In 1977, the Ganleys returned to Peterborough and began to draw people interested in supporting poor people's projects in Jamaica, both urban and rural.

The Ganleys were then off to Dar-es-Salaam, Tanzania on another CIDA posting from 1978-1981, but the seed of Jamaican Self-Help had been planted, and it became incorporated as a registered charity and NGO in 1980. In 1985, the YWCA of Peterborough named Rosemary Ganley "Woman of the Year."

To her delight, the award was presented by her favorite Canadian writer, Margaret Laurence. The two women shared a deep admiration for Caribbean literature, and for peace and justice activism. Rosemary studied Caribbean literature at the University of the West Indies, and African literature later at the University of Dar-es-Salaam, Tanzania.

Rosemary's interest were broad - internationalism and the role of religions from a feminist perspective were among them. She attended the United Nations Fourth World Conference on Women in Beijing in 1995. She and her colleague Linda Slavin founded the first Person's Day Breakfast in Peterborough in 1991.

Rosemary and John Ganley made frequent trips to Jamaica to strengthen links, monitor projects and encourage partners. They moved back to Jamaica in 1998 to rural Highgate, St. Mary, and lived there part of each year for three years. Rosemary taught feminist theology at the University of the West Indies.

The writing continued. Coming back to live in Canada, Rosemary commuted to Toronto from 2001 to 2006 as co-editor of the independent newspaper, *Catholic New Times*. Her volunteer work with Jamaican Self-Help was onging, and she accompanied some 600 youth to Jamaica on awareness trips from 1984-2012. In 2011, the Ganleys were added to the Peterborough Pathway of Fame, and in 2012 Rosemary was named a "Woman of Distinction" by the Red Pashmina Campaign. Rosemary currently writes a weekly column for the *Peterborough Examiner*.

Most recently, Rosemary Ganley was named by Prime Minster Trudeau to the Gender Equality Advisory Council for the G7 meetings in Canada in June, 2018.

Rosemary's email address is *rganley2016@gmail.com*

For updates and purchasing books online, please see
www.yellowdragonflypress.ca

95891144R00135

Made in the USA
Columbia, SC
21 May 2018